ARKANA

ONE CONTINUOUS MISTAKE

Gail Sher's expertise crosses several disciplines. She was named Teacher of the Year by the combined Education Faculties of University of California at Berkeley, Stanford, and San Francisco State University and has taught classes in writing, psychology, and Zen on the graduate-school level for many years. She also leads workshops and ongoing groups for writers.

As a psychotherapist she supervises and consults with individuals and couples.

Her first published book, *From a Baker's Kitchen* (1984), based on her work as the founding baker of (the now famous) Tassajara Bread Bakery, attracted national attention. *The Bloomsbury Review* said, "The text is resplendent with words that will tempt and encourage you." Technical writers praised its organization and clarity and Catherine Fredman of Diversion named it as one of the "Year's Ten Best Baking Books."

Since then she has published eight books of avant-garde poetry, three book-length haiku sequences, as well as poems and haiku in over twenty literary journals (some have won awards). Along with regularly lecturing and giving poetry readings throughout the United States, this year she was elected to be listed in the ninth edition of the *International Who's Who in Poetry and Poets' Encyclopaedia* published in Cambridge, England.

One Continuous Mistake

FOUR NOBLE TRUTHS FOR WRITERS

GAIL SHER

PENGUIN
ARKANA

ARKANA

Published by the Penguin Group
Penguin Putnam Inc., 375 Hudson Street,
New York, New York 10014, U.S.A.
Penguin Books Ltd, 27 Wrights Lane,
London W8 5TZ, England
Penguin Books Australia Ltd, Ringwood,
Victoria, Australia
Penguin Books Canada Ltd, 10 Alcorn Avenue,
Toronto, Ontario, Canada M4V 3B2
Penguin Books (N.Z.) Ltd, 182–190 Wairau Road,
Auckland 10, New Zealand

Penguin Books Ltd, Registered Offices:
Harmondsworth, Middlesex, England

First published in Arkana 1999

5 7 9 10 8 6 4

Grateful acknowledgment is made for permission to reprint an excerpt
from "Ripples on the Surface" from *No Nature* by Gary Snyder.
Copyright © 1992 by Gary Snyder. Reprinted by permission of
Pantheon Books, a division of Random House, Inc.

LIBRARY OF CONGRESS CATALOGING-IN-PUBLICATION DATA
Sher, Gail, 1942–
One continuous mistake: four noble truths for writers /
Gail Sher.
p. cm.
Includes bibliographical references.
ISBN 0 14 01.9587 4 (pbk.)
1. Authorship. I. Title.
PN145.S46 1999
808'.02—dc21   98–36537

Printed in the United States of America
Set in Bulmer
Designed by Kathryn Parise

For Brendan

ACKNOWLEDGMENTS

To properly acknowledge the forces that brought this book into being would require a directory of the universe. Still, a few individuals are noteworthy. First and foremost is prose-writer Merry White Benezra. Before her knowledge, perspicacity, wit, linguistic brio—not to mention her compassion for the uninitiated reader—all offered up in a spirit of tireless generosity—I stand in awe.

Kimn Nielson "saw" the title buried in an early draft. Debby Callaway did tons of leg work. Both I thank.

For my agent Sarah Jane Freymann's kindness, astuteness, concern and carefully modulated presence along with my editor Carole DeSanti's unfailing support, I am moved and honored.

To my Zen teacher, Shunryu Suzuki-roshi, and my guru, Paramahansa Yogananda, I bow with unmeasurable gratitude.

CONTENTS

Writing Saved My Life

Writing saved my life. Before I found writing I had exhausted all the other ways of being in the world that I knew about. But, as with anything that one makes entirely one's own, I had to reinvent writing. I had to unravel everything I had been taught and wind it back up again, *my* way.

Before I found writing, I longed for writing. In my earliest memory I am four and frustrated with my inability to have my words all gathered together on a piece of paper. Over the years frustration endlessly reinvented itself.

One version took the form of not writing. What can I write about? I'd think. Inflect this sentence four ways and you have the whole story. *What* can I write about? I have no subject. *Can?* I have no skill. *I?* Insignificant me? *Write about* implies savoring, highlighting, treasuring some aspect of my experience. But my experiences seemed small.

Another version was a disconcerting sense of being peripheral to my life. The activity that belonged to me (I felt sure) was writing but I couldn't find a way "in" to writing. I developed an intense nostalgia as if a precious possession (so familiar) was being mysteriously withheld from me.

The solution came via haiku (short unrhymed Japanese poems capturing the essence of a moment). For several years I wrote one haiku a day and then spent hours polishing those I had written on previous days. This tiny step proved increasingly satisfying.

Gradually it dawned on me that the healing factor was not the haiku but the "one per day." Without even knowing it, I had developed a "practice." Everyday, no matter what, I wrote one haiku. In my mind I became the person who writes "a haiku a day." That was the beginning of knowing who I was.

When my haiku-writing "period" turned into a generic "writing period," I was launched. The focus was on attendance—being present for writing. It really didn't matter *what* I wrote during that time.

Writing comes like an urge or a pulse, not to say something, but to be with words as they arise and then to shape them or craft them. The words could be wood. It makes no difference.

One beats through me, pushes its way to the forefront and appears on a page. I care about this. I care about the clarity of myself as a vessel, the utensils used, the paper as receptor and the way the whole process unfolds. Silence for me is replete with possibility.

Just at dusk I seat myself cross-legged in my wooden chair. Before me placemat-like is a square Japanese cloth upon which rests a quilted box holding all my writing utensils. I position my notebook on the cloth beside my skinny blue mechanical pencil and stick eraser. The pink eraser tip just emerges from its clear plastic sheath, oddly phallic.

I am surrounded by flat bare surfaces. I am straight-backed, warm, well-supported. I close my eyes and begin with a prayer. I relax into the luxury of here, the richness of the space, the soft light, the pure quiet.

My consciousness spins toward a vortex in the center of which is a word. It is mine and I write it down. I am steady, unperturbed. I have no feeling outside of this steadiness, a taut yet receptive state of being awake. Listening for the sound of a word I am totally still except for the slight motion of my hand guiding the pencil.

Part I

A WRITING "HABIT"

Facing fear, developing a one-pointed mind, nursing a writing "habit," cultivating daily writing periods, finding the middle way, and burning yourself completely—all belong to the "how" of regularity—to making writing a practice.

EXERCISE

Writing *Zazen*

Write on the same subject every day for two weeks. Revisiting the same subject day after day will force you to exhaust stale, inauthentic, spurious thought patterns and dare you to enter places of subtler, more "fringe" knowing.

FOUR NOBLE TRUTHS

FOR WRITERS

"It is not just the food in front of us, but our readiness to receive, to be blessed with food, that allows food to do its feeding," Ed Brown, Zen priest and master chef, astutely observes.

Just so. Our readiness to receive and to be blessed by our writing allows it to nourish us.

If you are a writer, you have probably noticed that when you are writing, it feels correct and that when you are not writing (when there is no room for writing in your life), it feels incorrect. When you write, you sit down with the intention to *be*. If you are a writer, writing and being are the same.

Of course we bring, each according to our temperament, more to it. Though each of our "mores" has a different flavor, all are somewhat extraneous to the practice aspect of writing.

Only "intention" is essential. When Ed Brown

says, "our readiness to receive," he's talking about intention.

The value of a vow (a "practice" is a vow—"I vow to have a writing period every day") is in perfecting its methodology. Issan Dorsey, a Zen priest at San Francisco Zen Center, used to say, "You don't clean to make things clean, so much. You clean even if it's not a mess. You just go around and make things look like somebody paid attention to them."[1]

Issan's advice is equally applicable to writing. Cleaning is not about achieving some once-and-for-all pristine state of immaculateness. Human beings clean. Writer's write. It is the most fundamental of the Four Noble Truths for writers.

1. Writers write.
2. Writing is a process.
3. You don't know what your writing will be until the end of the process.
4. If writing is your practice, the only way to fail is to not write.

POINTING DIRECTLY AT YOUR OWN HEART, YOU'LL FIND BUDDHA

> *There is no Shakespeare; there is no Beethoven; certainly and emphatically there is no God; we are the words; we are the music; we are the thing itself.*
>
> —VIRGINIA WOOLF[2]

Writing is infinite, ever elusive and ungraspable. We can never know what writing is. We can only know our experience minute to minute, as we write.

A great psychoanalyst used to say that each clinical hour should begin "without memory, without desire, without understanding." The intentional remembering of a previous session (holding the person to who she was in the past), the desire (to cure or influence), and the illusion of understanding, all contend against the kind of receptivity that allows something entirely new to arise. The underlying principle is that the unconscious does the work. The healing factor is the power of the person's psyche, given the right support, to resolve its own conflicts. The psychoanalyst is witness to the person's inherent healing power just as a writer, if she generates the space, can witness her inherent creative power. The main job is to be there, but out of the way.

The principle "Be there but out of the way," a hallmark of Zen monasteries, is instilled in its students by means of a daily schedule. When you arrive, you are told what to do. Then you just show up, day after day, putting one foot in front of the other.

At least your body does. Your mind may run an ongoing commentary, asking questions, bebopping around, liking it, hating it, to the point of exhaustion.

This is practice—monitoring your state-of-mind as projected onto the "blank screen" of a repeated activity. Since the "practice" is set (in our case, writing practice), any variation will be a reflection of *you*. The mantra (mindset) "without memory, without desire, without understanding" flourishes in this, its natural environment, lending you the openness to be entirely "there but out of the way"—in the throes of your self, your self-awareness and your indefatigable spirit.

SINGLE-MINDED

EFFORT

"Perseverance furthers." The *I Ching* validates small, easily-discounted accomplishments. Cumulatively, "slow but steady" works, not only for writing but for body building, saving money, gardening, sewing a quilt.

John Stevens, Professor of Buddhist Studies and Aikido Instructor in Sendai, Japan, describes the practice of a *gyōja* (spiritual athlete) who runs a 100-day stretch of *kaihōgyō*, a 52.5 mile marathon on Japan's sacred Mount Hiei. Each "daily" run begins at midnight with an hour-long service in the Buddha Hall and is completed between 7:30 and 9:30 A.M. depending on weather conditions and how conscientiously the prayers and offerings along the way are performed. The gyōja wears a uniform of pure-white cotton. A "cord of death" with a sheathed knife tucked inside loops around his waist. Should the gyōja fail to complete a single portion of the practice on any one night, he vows to kill himself.

No matter what. This is the first aspect of single-minded effort. If you take on writing as your practice, to recognize that writing *is* your practice, you need to have the attitude "write or die." Not because you "should," but because if writing *is* your practice, if you don't write, you will feel something terribly important is missing from your life—and nothing, including prayer, meditation, exercise, money or love will make up for it.

Plodding onward is the second aspect of single-minded effort. The poet John Ashbery once told an interviewer, "It's important to try to write when you are in the wrong mood or the weather is wrong. Even if you don't succeed you'll be developing a muscle that may do it later on."

His Holiness the Dalai Lama (in a 1994 class series) said that when his formal study of Buddhism began at age six, he had no interest in Buddhism, but around age sixteen, his interest perked up. About thirty-five, he began to feel that he was making progress. In his forties, he made more progress but did not have entire *bodhicitta* (an enlightened mind). It makes him want to laugh, he said, when he meets people who attain realization in a short time. We might think that the Dalai Lama would be exempt from such effort, but he insists that single-minded effort, the plodding, day-after-day kind, is necessary for everyone.

A third aspect of single-minded effort is its wake of deep satisfaction. I know a doctor who wishes he could teach literature. I know a lawyer who secretly writes children stories. I don't know any writer, however, who hankers after an alternative profession. If you are a writer and you are writing, there may be problems but never doubt.

GRANDMOTHER'S

FINGERPOINTING [3]

*Make writing your practice . . . If you commit
to it, writing will take you as deep as Zen.*
—KATAGIRI-ROSHI

It is shocking how the tiniest vow, taken seriously,
can throw you into a situation similar to that of the
Buddha during the night of his enlightenment. The
temptations to break your vow ("I will have a regular
daily writing period.") come at you from every angle.
Thoughts such as "What's to be gained? What difference will it make? I'm never going to amount to
anything as a writer anyway" flood your mind.
Wouldn't it make more "sense" to just answer the
door, answer the phone, and get on with your day?

In fact, what is there to support *not* getting on
with your day? Logic, the world, your partner and

family all cry out for you to break your vow to write. It only takes a moment to assure yourself that your vow to write for, say, twenty minutes, is ridiculous.

Probably you will arrive at this critical juncture every single day. Do not deceive yourself into thinking that once you "get it down" or once you "clear out" your life or next month or next year things will be different. Every single day (for me after twenty years it is still every single day) your mind will offer an exceedingly good reason not to have a writing period.

But . . . writers write. If you can't get to the paper, writing won't occur.

In addition to contributing to the development of self-discipline and self-knowledge, an unmissable daily writing period offers something even more vital to a writer—emphasis on attendance. If the emphasis is on attendance, one has marvelously succeeded as soon as one is seated at one's desk. So long as one is present and task-focused, one needn't necessarily *write* a word. One's commitment is solely to *attend* and if writing doesn't happen, then that's what "happened" in one's writing period. Consequently one is free to allow *anything* to happen and herein lies the beauty of this approach. The unimaginable, unthinkable, the utterly original has room to emerge.

One year I lived alone in a colorful old Berkeley apartment. The plumbing in the building was ancient and this day the cumulative effect of months, perhaps decades, of leakage from upstairs finally resulted in the collapse of my studio's ceiling. Plaster and pipe water were everywhere. A cold drizzly night was approaching and I hadn't yet had a writing period. I thought, "The sky is falling but I haven't had a writing period. First I'll have a writing period. Then I'll deal with the sky."

Writing *is* lonely. Anything you do entirely is lonely because *you* have to do it. You can get advice, instruction, support, love, but in the end, no one can else can show up, day after day, at your desk.

MAKING WRITING PERIODS SUCCESSFUL AND ENJOYABLE

- Do not reread the writing from your writing period until another time, preferably another day, when you can do so with objectivity. Ideally you might set aside one day per week solely for revising, a separate skill, best done on a separate occasion.

- If the peripheral aspects of your life are not managed properly, you risk arriving at your desk and proceeding to doze or, worse, problem-solve. If you are serious about writing, you will find that your entire life, even the smallest aspects of it, must be organized around this desire.

- Before you begin each writing session, dedicate your writing and your intention to write. Offer up the effort and the fruit of this effort so that it no longer belongs to you.

- Outside of insuring that they happen, don't plan your writing periods. Use your will to punctually attend them, not to control what happens once you get there. Obsessing about the latter is a time-honored way to intimidate you out of going. The beauty of writing periods is the emphasis on "how" over "what."

- It's okay to have a soothing drink along with your writing period. Preparing coffee or tea, for example, can become part of your pre-writing ritual. The anticipation and pleasure of drinking it will serve your larger purpose.

- With all due respect to those people who are energized by the haphazard and chaotic, most would-be writers will benefit from setting up a "place" for their writing. Any activity performed with intensity is best done in an area specifically designated for that activity. This way all one's tools are there and the vibrations from previous cumulative efforts will support your efforts in the moment.

I can't help writing—so there's an end of it.
—VIRGINIA WOOLF

When Flannery O'Connor's writing was successful, it was thanks to her "novelist's habit." Kenzabura Oë, the Nobel Prize winner for Literature, says, "and I am sure it is the same accumulated practice that [helps any artist] reveal a landscape no one has seen before."

Sally Fitzgerald, editor of O'Connor's collected letters, notes that in addition to O'Connor's "novelist's habit"

. . . she acquired as well, I think, a second distinguished habit, which I have called "the habit of being:" an excellence not only of action but of interior disposition and activity that increasingly reflected. . . . in what she did and said.[4]

Oë's "novelist's habit" plus Fitzgerald's "habit of being" add up to what I am calling "writing practice"—attending regular daily writing periods with an alert, receptive mind. Perhaps it should be called a writing "habit."

Without consciously intending it, Ralph Waldo Emerson had a writing habit:

> He wrote constantly, he wrote about everything, he covered hundreds of pages. When he had nothing to say, he wrote about having nothing to say. He read and indexed and reread what he had written. He copied letters into his journals and prose from his journals into his letters. He laughed at much of it when he read it over, inserting comments such as "dead before it reached its subject," but he kept at it.[5]

Henry David Thoreau did, too:

> It was becoming a habit with him now to work back over his journals and to reread books, to reengage old subjects in the light of new interests, to revise and recopy his own earlier journal work, measuring, weighing, culling, and sorting his materials. He continually reached backward. . . . taking up earlier

threads, reweaving and combining them. . . . searching out what it was in each that made it of lasting rather than passing interest.[6]

Virginia Woolf constantly monitored the timetable of her workday, congratulating or reproaching herself on how well she kept to her "work account." She variously asserted, "Habit is the desirable thing in writing" or "What one wants for writing is habit."

Thomas Merton, the Christian mystic, once told a friend (referring to his writing "habit") that he needed to write "just to stay sane."

A habit is the link between inspiration and self-realization. Sometimes the hardest part of an undertaking is not when you start out (you have your initial enthusiasm) and not as you near the end (you have the anticipation of being almost finished) but the middle when your motivation dwindles and all that you seemingly have is your resolution. That's enough. "We are what we repeatedly do," Aristotle said. "Excellence . . . is not an act, but a habit."

WAVES OF THE SEA

BELONG TO THE SEA

Because "poetry is a way of celebrating the actuality of a nondual universe in all its facets," Gary Snyder calls an accomplished poem "a kind of gift exchange in the mind-energy webs." Bashō, the seventeenth-century Japanese haiku-master, considered all poetry and art offerings to the Buddha.

Some years ago I consulted a Tibetan Rinpoche (Rinpoche is a title, literally meaning "precious one," given to a lama who is recognized incarnation of a past revered teacher.) about my use of regular daily writing periods as a form of meditation. I expected him to tell me that I must meditate (in the traditional sense) and that perhaps the initiatory rites of Tibetan Buddhism would be sustaining and cleansing. Instead, he gently advised, "Dedicate. Before you write and after you write, make sure to give it away." He further suggested that I dedicate everything I do, not just writing. I'd like to, but I forget. With writing, however, I do not forget. The single act of dedication has transformed my writing practice.

For writing practice to be complete, we must give it away: the effort, the results, and identification with the results. Much of the happiness that total absorption in an activity brings is nullified by the belief that it is ours—that we know what we are doing. But anything we hold onto causes disharmony.

Dedicating your writing and your efforts to write resituates your primary intention within a larger context. You become a vessel through which creative spirit flows. Without this resituation (letting-go), one leaves tracks.

Whether it be a story, a poem, a haiku, a letter, words go beyond the wordless essence when they (as a refuge and a way) no longer belong to you.

WRITING POSTURE

These forms are not the means of obtaining the right state of mind. To take this posture is itself to have the right state of mind. There is no need to obtain some special state of mind.
— Shunryu Suzuki-roshi

As soon as you bend your back, you lose power. Even if it's just at the beginning of your writing period, if you can sit comfortably with your spine straight, it will ground you. Your writing will be more alive because it will come from a place of greater self-connection.

The adjustments are simple. Fold your legs in front of your couch and use a pillow to support the small of your back. In bed, position yourself upright instead of prone, and use a back-pillow and lap-desk for additional support. Sit cross-legged (meditation style) at your desk or use a "kneeler" to automatically stabilize your posture. (Some writers are able to maintain a straight back in a normal sitting position using an ordinary chair.) Even in the middle of the kitchen floor, you can sit *seiza* (calves folded under thighs). Or use a lectern and write standing up. Virginia Woolf did. You may have a breakthrough in your writing standing at your dresser!

EXPERIMENTING WITH POSTURES

Try writing with your spine relaxed but straight (make sure your body is in an otherwise comfortable position) and again with your spine intentionally curved. Notice how the energy from your *hara* (navel) is cut off when your back bends. It pools in the head which can lead to flat, stale writing. (There may be times when you *want* to come from your head.) The point is to know your body and what it needs at any particular moment to write to your highest specifications.

THE KISS OF THE ASP

Describing the bell-ringing ritual that precedes *do-kusan* (a private interview with a Zen teacher), Philip Kapleau-roshi says:

> . . . *how* the bell is struck tells the roshi, who can hear the sound in his room, whether the student is a beginner or a more advanced student and what the condition of his or her mind is.

"How" we do anything tells us the same thing.

"Always do what you are afraid to do," Ralph Waldo Emerson's visionary Aunt Mary advised him. We tie ourselves in knots to sabotage the energy that might be unleashed if we move resolutely ahead. The risks of making changes are great . . . especially great changes.

Actually, the risks of not making changes are great. We risk missing our lives.

Sometimes writers don't move resolutely ahead because they fear that once they start, they'll never stop.

Like an anorexic who refuses to eat because her hunger is so deep, if she lets herself, she could eat forever—well, couldn't she? If a writer finally lets herself write, without any artificial boundaries, couldn't she write forever?

Yet there is a difference between addiction and practice. Regarding God, for example, Paramahansa Yogananda said, "It's okay to be addicted [to God]." "It's okay to be addicted to God" means that it's okay to use the energy that drives an addiction to fuel one's personal relationship with God because the latter will not (as a true addiction will) drain the psyche; rather, it will fill it. Writing will also.

Korean Zen Master Soen-sa-nim was adamant. "Zen means believing in yourself one hundred percent." To do so requires knowing yourself, standing up for yourself, "owning" your fears and weaknesses. This is hard for a writer—to keep owning her fears and to still write. If you try to tackle it with your mind alone, you're likely to stop writing.

Yet succumbing to fear is worse than taking on the thing feared. It removes you from reality by creating an artificial focus. You waste your strength fighting an endlessly elusive battle. Derailed, tipped off-center, you walk through your days like a ghost.

The solution for a writer who fears she will never

stop writing once she starts is simply to attend daily writing periods. The beauty of writing periods is that they have a beginning and an end. You attend them and that's all.

We say we aren't writing (listening to ourselves) in the name of consideration for others. But this is a false premise because we can't listen to others (really) until we learn to listen, exquisitely listen, and *to abide by* our own heart.

THE WRITER'S

MIDDLE WAY

Writers are always writing whether they are writing or not. You are either writing or doing what you need to do in order to write—paying bills, buying supplies, going to the dentist. It takes all day.

Thus the pull to abuse, to go overboard or underboard. How does a writer figure out the correct regimen, the writer's middle way?

Little Girls in Pretty Boxes, by Joan Ryan, is an exposé of the suffering and exploitation endured by elite gymnasts and ice skaters, typically children under fifteen, often under twelve. Training as much as nine hours a day, prepubescent girls adhere to a male-inspired routine. No consideration is given to the effect of their regime on bone density, forthcoming menstrual cycles, eating patterns (starvation patterns) and low self-esteem. There is a driven quality about their coaches who feel they are fighting a losing battle with time.

The girls themselves are taught to let neither their pain nor feelings show. They perform with broken bones and torn ligaments. Coaches wangle doctors into lying about their gymnasts' need for rest and medicine so that the show (upon which the *coach's* reputation is based) will go on. Through overuse and undernourishment, some of these children's bones resemble those of post-menopausal women.

The drive to perfection is intensely powerful. In the case of gymnasts, ice skaters and anorexics, this drive can lead to death. Before his enlightenment, Buddha was also tempted to extremes. Afterwards he taught the middle way.

What precisely is the middle way? If you absolutely love chocolate-chip cookies, you can go to Mrs. Field's and pig out or you can forbid yourself ever to touch a chocolate chip (since you know you can't restrain yourself). The middle way is to have two. It's the hardest way because you can't just bliss out and die in chocolate-chip heaven and you can't use rigidity (some very strict rule) to keep yourself from experiencing how delicious chocolate-chip cookies are. You have to taste (feel) everything—their scrumptiousness, and also that your body can handle only two at a time. You have to stay conscious.

Each situation has its own middle way. Every minute is a new situation. Writers must become Olympians of middle-way points.

At best it is difficult. When a study found that swimmers who swim 10,000 yards a day perform no better than those who swim half that distance, coaches still wanted their swimmers to swim 10,000. How does one resist the enticement toward the familiar? No one can tell you. *You* have to figure it out . . . again and again.

Before figuring it out you must *want* to figure it out. After figuring it out you must demonstrate the courage to say "no" to the forces all around you that will tempt you away. Universities, corporations, the media, spiritual authorities, even friends and family will push you to squelch the part of you that *knows*. A tremendous amount of consciousness is required to stay with your hard-earned understanding.

Katagiri-roshi taught that it's not important whether a spiritual teacher has reached his peak or not. It only matters whether he has digested the truth he has experienced. Thorough digestion takes time and care, consciousness and commitment. Lastly, it takes a fine-tuned instinct for the middle way—the right regimen, day after day, so you can continue with it endlessly.

DISTRACTIONS

*Just when the author sits down to write, "the
monster of grim commonsense" will lumber up
the steps "to whine that the book is not for the
general public, that the book will never
never—And right then, just before it blurts
out the word s, e, double-l, false commonsense
must be shot dead."*[7]

—VLADIMIR NABOKOV

We all face distractions. Common ones for writers
are envy (mental comparisons), fear, boredom, and
low self-esteem. However, looked at properly, every
distraction can be turned into an opportunity to intensify and sharpen our writing practice.

Even if you faithfully attend your writing periods,
when you start comparing yourself (to other writers,
to an ideal or arbitrary standard), you lose power—
self-referential power. Staying with one's practice
means to stay with who you are right now. "I feel

that as a writer I have something to say, but. . . ."
But? But what? Stay with this "but" until you are,
about "but," the most knowledgeable person in the
world.

Your reaction to another person's "success" or
"failure" may show you something you may not have
been able to acknowledge about your desires. Envy
is like a wail—"Hey, what about *me?*" Use it as a
wake-up call. You *do* need to be more mindful of
your aspirations and how to achieve them.

Writing-related fear and low self-esteem both arise
from straying attention. Sometimes the person is
seeking an inappropriate (unrealistic) result. If a beginning writer is riveted on the praise and attention
she will receive from "good writing," her writing
(based on wobbly concentration) will lack the very
quality that would bring her the acceptance for which
she yearns. Her desire to be brilliant redirects itself
toward the idea of success based on another person's
opinion over which she has little control (herein lies
the basis for fear) rather than toward the commitment
to make consistent effort—over which she has total
control.

If you are bored, your mind is wandering—away
from you—its rightful focus. That "not a yard of
cloth can be woven without the most thorough fi-

delity in the weaver" is as true for writers as it is for weavers, however differing their *expression* of "fidelity."

Shortly after Rick Fields, poet, writer and student of Chögyam Trungpa Rinpoche, was diagnosed with lung cancer, he attended a Medicine Buddha teaching. When you have a sickness, the Tibetan lama said, affirm to yourself, "May this sickness help me take on the sickness of all other people who are suffering in the same way so that they will be free from their suffering." This is the approach of a bodhisattva.

The Tibetan lama turned everything around—just like *you* can turn everything around when you feel bored, afraid, jealous or bad about yourself. When Thomas Merton says, "If you have never had any distractions you don't know how to pray" he means that an unchallenged concentration is probably a shallow one.

Staying focused on who you are (with all your faults) requires maturity, perseverance and tremendous self-compassion. Act like and treat yourself as though your mind were joyful, kind and big—as though it were radiant, unlimitedly friendly and large. In reality, your true nature is such and if you treat yourself this way, you just may rise to the occasion.

Part II

LIKE JESUS,
IT'S FROM GOD.
AND FROM YOU.

Invest in what supports the process: stay-at-home days, reading, capturing fleeting thoughts, paring down, revision time.

Writing *Kinhin*

Kinhin is slow walking meditation (about a half-step per breath) usually practiced for short periods between longer periods of sitting meditation as a means of refreshing one's body, mind and spirit.

Practice *kinhin* in a setting of your choice, then write about what you noticed. Gradually (ideally) you will be able to skip the formal *kinhin* part and simply see everything in your daily life (*and* write about it) with a *kinhin* mind.

STAY-AT-HOME DAYS

We can travel a long way and do many dif-
ferent things, but our deepest happiness is not
born from accumulating new experiences. It is
born from letting go of what is unnecessary,
and knowing ourselves to be always at home.
— SHARON SALZBURG

"Stay-at-home days with, apparently at least, 'noth-ing' to do are bread and butter for a writer, our most indispensable sort of days," asserts Kenzaburo Oë. Emerson is emphatic about his views on staying put: "They who made England, Italy or Greece venerable in the imagination," did so not by traveling, but "by sticking fast where they were, like an axis of the Earth."

Emerson once tried to raise money to help his transcendentalist friend, Ellery Channing, go to Europe because Ellery insisted that seeing buildings, and pictures, and mountains, and peasantries must be part of his poetic education. However, while Channing was away, Thoreau, at home, learned that the history of a man who spends his days in the library may be as interesting as the "Peninsular campaigns."

"A writer's country is a territory within his own brain; and we run the risk of disillusionment if we try to turn such phantom cities into tangible brick and mortar," comments Virginia Woolf.[8]

Home is where writing happens. The writer's desk is a miniature world. Self-contained. Hopefully quiet. Anywhere else is somewhere else.

Could it be Beelzebub who wafts these evanescent messages up from the underworld? One is set adrift, ethereal, mercurial—"I was thinking about something entirely different . . ." or "Apropos of nothing . . ." or "I don't even think this way but it struck me . . ." or "Out of the blue the word 'flub' began ringing in my ears."

Last night's dream floats into consciousness. The setting is terribly familiar . . . as if all one's dreams are different episodes enacted on a migratory stage.

In a plant, the compounds within an oil molecule are protected by a diaphanous membrane. Toward evening the oil rises to the surface. In the morning the sun's warmth relaxes the membrane, which opens and releases the oil into the atmosphere. If the membrane is fractured while the oil is being released, the oil is damaged and its molecular structure changed.

Raindrop Therapy is a process of dribbling the

oils like little drops of rain from about six inches above the body. Drip . . . drip . . . drip. Each trickle brings its own small shock to the body-part.

Fleeting thoughts, like essence-of-oil raindrops, quietly shock our being. You think one. Sometimes it's so gentle you don't even realize it's there.

But it *is* there (momentarily) and because it *has been* there, your mind contains the memory. And there is the cumulative effect of its presence juxtaposed with other subtle presences. Drip . . . drip . . . drip. Your consciousness is no longer the same.

You are no longer the same. A fleeting thought may be fleeting but its impact is forever.

Just as you keep track of your philosophical thoughts, your spiritual thoughts, your pecuniary thoughts and thoughts of your loved ones, thoughts that flicker through the interstices of your consciousness are equally compelling if *you* are your main tool.

CAPTURING THEM

Rich and insightful though they may be, fleeting thoughts are transient. Vagabonds of the mind, they appear then disappear. Writers must catch these volatile vapors. "How do you do *that?*" (We have dream-catchers, how 'bout fleeting-thought catchers?)

Writers carry notebooks. Some writers carry notebooks in which they never jot things down but anyway they carry them. Then one day there is an explosion of understanding. The old notebook is right there.

I know a writer who ties a rope around her notebook and wears it like a backpack all day long.

Writers carry dictaphones or tiny tape recorders or index cards or post-it notes. Or they simply carry a pencil and are alert to the whereabouts of napkins, matchbook covers, bits of debris.

A good book *is* you. That's why you can't put it down.

A good reader co-writes every book she reads. You and your friend can never read the same book because what *you* make up behind and during the reading will be entirely different from the imaginings of your friend. If you try to reread the same book, you can't. You will have been changed by the first run through.

Like writing, reading is organic. "It was a disappointment to realize that they were actually written by people, that books were not natural wonders, coming up of themselves like grass," Eudora Welty admits. Snippets of thought, speech, dreams, melody are woven together bit by tiny bit and sometimes unwoven and rewoven again and again before the thing is done. Even then it is not done. Each reader carries on the process. (Virginia Woolf calls this the "after reading.") Insofar as a reader bestows a part of her self to the finished product she is purged.

. . . yet this only is reading, in a high sense, not that which lulls us as a luxury and suffers the nobler faculties to sleep the while, but what we have to stand on tiptoe to read and devote our most alert and wakeful hours to.

—Henry David Thoreau,
from *Walden*

Reading that is physically, emotionally and intellectually strenuous can be just as demanding as writing. Words are sovereign. To open one's mind, heart and spirit one must be present to them—self-forgetfully immersed. *You* become an open book in order to read one properly.

Therefore the value of rubbish. We can't always be reading *King Lear*. Our psyche needs rest and afterwards to prepare for the feat. Junk reading, like junk food, can be adventurous, morale-boosting.

Ephemera are "the dressing-rooms, the workshops, the wings, the sculleries, the bubbling cauldrons, where life seethes and steams and is for ever on the boil."[9] Trashy novels, run-of-the-mill mysteries, obscure biographies, the latest "zines" plunk us down in a public reality that cushions and offsets the rare, exotic, exquisite yet painfully isolating masterpiece.

READING SUPPORTS

WRITING —

BUT WATCH OUT!

I know someone who reads voraciously and is stimulated by his books' many ideas, but when he closes them, his mind is swimming. Instead of unleashing his creative energies (he aspires to become a writer), his books act as a drug, lulling him to escape.

He tells himself that at least he is reading and that reading is related to writing. The truth is that the *way* he reads—dreamlike and with little methodology—leaves him ungrounded. Without knowing it, he "abuses" reading, using reading to avoid the terror of, instead of as an anchor for, his ambition to write.

Reading provides proximity to language. If you are writing about trees, you can bathe your consciousness in tree-related material to create a pool from which your unconscious may sip when you still yourself.

But while reading supports writing, it might also be a dodge. Writing is active, reading can be passive. The relaxed interaction with language that much reading provides, outside of the context of a regular writing practice, can encourage an "I'll-think-about-that-tomorrow" stance toward the more cumbersome task of writing. Because reading creates a slight trance state, it even has the potential to be addictive. Time goes by and little else seems to get accomplished. Even the *desire* for accomplishment is numbed. Living vicariously through the thoughts and feelings of book characters, it is easy to forget one intended to be a writer in the first place!

In his biography of Ralph Waldo Emerson, Robert D. Richardson, Jr., reports:

Sometimes the books of a month of Emerson's life are merely an inventory of a month's distractions. Anyone can amass an impressive amount of reading. But the active filtration and the tight focus of constant intention which convert that reading into real life experience and then into adequate expression, these are the exclusive properties of the great writer.[10]

A writer sifts his reading through his emotional, psychological, spiritual and aesthetic experience, transmuting it into language that is his own. This in itself is stabilizing. Instead of floating around on effervescent clouds of disappearing thoughts, he gradually becomes rooted in his own approach, his own vision and imagination. Even if he just writes a paragraph, he will "have" something from which he can build. Money isn't the only commodity subject to the "power of compounding."

BLEACHED-BONE

SIMPLICITY

The Japanese poet Takamura Kotaro has said that an image of a person may look more authentic than the person himself because the person is distracted by what is not inherently his own life. "A living person has residues," Kotaro explains. "He possesses things that are not his molecules, things that are nonessential, ambivalent, and wasteful."[11]

In Japan the word *O-Sya-Re* carries the connotation of dressing up in order to make something look nicer. Etymologically, however, *O-Sya-Re,* composed of *Re* (to drop) and *Sya* (to dazzle), means to eliminate excess or overstatement. In this sense it reflects the old Japanese concept of beauty, which, emphasized "dressing *down*" to reveal an object's inherent virtue and loveliness.

We all know that paring down can be immensely satisfying. To be successful, however, we need to have criteria according to which we decide what to keep and what to eliminate. Such criteria presupposes self-knowledge.

Like a pump (which often brings up muddy water before it brings up clean), a writer (who is a kind of pump for her own personal purifying process), must be intimate with the mechanism—the pressure, the speed, the viscosity—that brings forth her best work and must be patient enough to wade through the muck that inevitably precedes it.

Suzuki-roshi taught that "excess" can even include making a special effort to achieve something. Just doing something without a particular effort, he said, is enough. Returning day after day to your writing period, not to achieve something, but to resume your writing nature, is a way to minimize "residues." (Attending your writing period *is* your writing nature.) As you begin to edit out the "nonessential, ambivalent, and wasteful," your writing style too will glow with inherent virtue and loveliness.

*. . . [Nabokov's] "best novels would be those
which he had to set aside for some time between the initial impulse and its ultimate realization. In the case of* The Defense, The
Gift, Lolita, Pale Fire, *and* Ada, *he would
start and finish another novel in the gap between his first idea and actual composition."*[12]

Muscles grow between times of maximum stress.
Bread dough rises between kneadings. The real work
of psychotherapy happens between regular scheduled
sessions. And, according to British psychoanalyst
D. W. Winnicott, creativity is fostered in transitional
space, the place in the psyche where inner and outer
come together.

Just as crowding a piece of writing pushes the
reader out, leaving insufficient room for the reader's
own associations, crowding the writing process

pushes a part of the writer out—often the vital part that suddenly "sees" the unimaginable, the unthinkable, the never-before conceived.

While the image of a writer in the throes of an idea (consumed, concentrated, riveted) is familiar to the point of cliché, we hardly ever hear about the time, toward the end of the writing process, when a writer (ideally) lets her writing rest . . . when she allows it to "just sit" (like in *zazen*) seemingly doing nothing.

But as anyone who has tried to do it knows, *zazen* is not nothing. Likewise, while one's writing sits, far from nothing, within the writer

everything flows together: colors and shapes and sounds and smells . . . ancient memories, recent impressions, immediate observations, future recollections; inside and outside, body and soul, self and other, individual reverie and family tension.[13]

Insects, butterflies, turtles, humans—their birth processes all include a gestation period. While we honor it in a moth, we forget about it in productions of our own invention. Or more accurately, we neglect to remember. Students, for example, notoriously stay up all night to "finish" a paper due the following day. No one, however, stays up all night to prepare a paper for its drawer (its rightful penultimate destination).

THE RUBBERY TIME

OF REVISION

> *. . . That special space that writing and re-
> writing afford just outside time. . . .*
>
> —Vladimir Nabokov

It took Gustave Flaubert one year to write eighty, perhaps ninety, pages of *Madame Bovary*. A runner can understand. For those who run marathons, often what stands out is not the marathon but preparing for the marathon—the staggered training, building up their bodies incrementally. Step by tiny step is how a city gets built. "Rome" is after-the-fact.

Coinciding with an outer process (a routine or writing "habit") is an inner process of broadening, intensifying, exploring the subtler implications of your original insight. Through the prism of your re-visionist's eye you may spot a refraction (perhaps THE critical discovery) that previously eluded you.

Or, like Ivan Sergeyevich Turgenev, it can be a "long struggle of elimination." Turgenev "wrote and re-wrote" to clear the truth of the unessential.

At the height of his fame Nabokov refused to be interviewed. He would only answer questions submitted in advance to which he could prepare written answers. As a writer, he said, all he had was the way he put things. He was intensely aware of the difference between his spoken language ("I speak like a child") and what he could achieve given the "rubbery time of revision."

ONE CONTINUOUS

MISTAKE

> *Finding out how to cook or how to work with others is something that comes with doing it, feeling your way along. And the more you master your craft, the more you know that the way is to keep finding out the way, not by just doing what you are already good at, but by going off into the darkness.*
>
> —ED ESPE BROWN[14]

Prayer is the soul talking to God (unadorned, unpretentious). Doing anything with wholehearted effort, which will likely involve mistake after mistake, is the soul talking to God in a different tongue.

"What does this have to do with writing?" you might ask.

Ralph Waldo Emerson noted, "There is no strong

performance without a little fanaticism in the performer. It is the men who are never contented who carry their point." Try again. Fail better. This is Samuel Beckett's writing instruction.

Writers tend to strive for perfection. Some say that the desire to be perfect is an expression of the desire to be one with God. However, it is important, and just as spiritual, to be aware of how one actually is. The effort to stay centered in one's self, minute after minute, is what Dogen Zenji, the Patriarch of Soto Zen, meant when he said Zen practice is one continuous mistake.

"In continuous practice, under a succession of agreeable and disagreeable situations, you will realize the marrow of Zen and acquire its true strength," Suzuki-roshi stressed. Jung adds an encouraging spin. We learn nothing from our successes, he says emphatically, which simply prescribe business-as-usual. We learn everything from our mistakes, which require us to analyze where we went wrong and invent fresh strategies.

When Issan Dorsey (who later became a Zen roshi) asked his teacher, Suzuki-roshi, for lay ordination, he said, "Roshi, I was going to come here and ask you if I could become your disciple. . . . Now I realize that that was just an ego trip on my part. So I'm going to keep on practicing and just do the best I can." Suzuki-roshi replied, "Well, there is no difference between that and being my disciple."[15]

LIKE JESUS,

IT'S FROM GOD.

AND FROM YOU.

Beginning writers are wont to confuse the "rush" that they feel in an inspired moment with "good" writing. In fact, if you use exhilaration as a criteria, you are likely to seek more of that and reject the concept of regular writing periods. If you can only write when the "spirit" moves you, you can hardly expect the spirit to move you on demand.

The spirit moving you tells you that you're onto something. Good writing, however, is the result of 1. being onto something; 2. distilling it through your internal purification process; 3. aging it; 4. seasoning it; 5. ciphoning off the fizz; 6. allowing the body to mellow, relax, mature until, by a kind of literary parthenogenesis, it gives birth to the other-than-you—to what you never expected, predicted, *could have thought up*. Like Jesus, it's from God. And from you.

The part from God is inexplicable. The part from you is developed skill. By working on writing you will develop a facility. Yes. Even you. Not in big moments, but little by little. That's how writing becomes yours.

"If only, somehow, Julia Roberts could be as complicated on-screen as the feelings she prompts in one
who looks carefully at her career." Ping! In a beau-
tifully crafted opening line David Thomson captures
the depth of his frustration, pinpoints Julia Robert's
real professional weakness, voices her fans' resulting
disappointment and introduces a thought-provoking
Movieline article on an actor whose real talent perhaps has not quite fully ripened.

"Ping"—the immediate recognition of a truth suddenly grasped and aptly conveyed—is a quality writers work hard to achieve. Embedded in David
Thompson's sentence is (undoubtedly) draft after
draft of the slightly-off. He had to 1. figure out the
psychology not only of Julia Roberts but of her admirers (himself included); 2. analyze their interaction
with her career; 3. infuse the results in his consciousness and patiently let them steep; until 4. out came
the distilled essence in twenty-three flowing words.

Language carries both unconscious and conscious

meaning. Writing can't ping until the two are integrated. When you hack away at your writing and it refuses to ping, it means you still have something to learn—either about your subject, your feelings about your subject, or, more likely, both.

Aesthetics have their own science whose unpindownable nature writers master. You must develop the you that "just knows" (your intuition) and stand unwaveringly by this knowledge. When someone asks for proof, just smile and say "because." "Ping" means "It's right and I know it."

Good writing happens cyclically, inside then outside, inside then outside. When it finally "pings," we simply bow.

FIVE PILLARS OF

WRITING

While some ingredients of "good writing" are elusive, others are clearly recognizable and lend themselves to conscientious application. I call these "pillars" because they are powerful, dependable and unfailingly supportive of good writing.

The five pillars illustrated here are elastic. As you experiment with them, you may find yourself emphasizing some and de-emphasizing others. The way you inflect the process will change depending on your needs.

A pillar is a mainstay. Its purpose is to support the structure of a unique creation. Position these invisible pillars in each and every writing project precisely where they will be of most help to you.

To demonstrate the pillars, let's apply them to the writing task "Use weather to convey a state of mind."

Pillar One:
Brainstorming

Brainstorming means allowing for anything. Your random thoughts, your calculated thoughts, your biases, fantasies, dreams, all are tributaries of you. Let them flow.

I love fog. I like to take long walks where there are lots of trees shrouded in mist and let my mind drift where it will. I like to be inside, very cozy, when it's raining. Lying down near an open window listening to a summer rain puts me instantly to sleep. Snow is amazing. A blanket of quiet coats the world. I feel so free when that happens. Of course my favorite is a sparkling winter morning—briskly going about in the crystal air. That is definitely my favorite. I do not relate to just plain sun. I would never take a sun-bath or play tennis or garden in the middle of the day if I could avoid it. I don't like extreme temperatures in either direction. That tiny town in Baja California where it's always over 100 degrees —I'd rather die than live there. And Chicago in February, yuk.

Omitting this stream of consciousness is often the cause of flat writing—writing where nothing unexpected, unpredictable, or wild occurs. Some writers prematurely push for closure, honing ideas before allowing them room to roam. Writing that is alive borders on what we don't know, don't understand, can't fathom. Letting words fall freely, without editing or censuring, puts us in touch with the unexpected in ourselves. That's where freshness comes from.

Pillar Two:
Journaling

Talk to yourself about what you will write. For example, after brainstorming, you might have the following internal monologue:

If I place in separate columns all the things I like about weather and all the things I dislike ("like" meaning a condition in which I feel connected with myself), a pattern emerges. All the things I like (fog, rain, snow, sparkling sun on a cold morning) interiorize me. All the things I dislike make me feel vacuous, false, lethargic, out of touch with my inner being. My strongest state is one in which I am most interior—alone, reflective, introspective—and certain weather conditions intensify this experience by deepening and prolonging it. I will write about a specific instance of feeling blissfully alone, sinking into an intimate relationship with myself as a result of the weather.

Whereas in Pillar One the point is "anything goes," in Pillar Two the point is to focus: to adopt an attitude/stance toward your subject. From your brainstorming session in Pillar One, for example, in Pillar Two you might just as easily have narrowed your topic to fog and written a story about a detective walking through a fog-bank mulling over a recent murder. Or you might suddenly have recalled the winter morning, years ago, when you hiked to a lake and mistook garbage on its opposite shore for penguins. Follow your energy, notice your proclivities and endorse a viewpoint. That's the essence of Pillar Two.

Pillar Three:
The Draft

Your draft will be a skeleton. The arm and leg bones will be recognizable, but they will still be no more than bones. Ideas will hang loosely together. Your job is to get what you have to say down on paper. Let it come. No obsessing. That happens later.

It had been a beautiful day, earlier, when I walked through the park to the oceanside theater. Having a few minutes to spare I took my latté to the outside section of the theater's little coffee shop so as to enjoy the fresh air and watch the other movie-goers grab a bite to eat before showtime. Their faces were filled with intelligence. While I relished my anonymity, in my heart, I felt a sisterhood with everyone I saw.

This is not the way I normally feel in a strange environment. The camaraderie, imagined or otherwise, was as nourishing as the film and the delicious espresso the theater prided itself on serving. But when the movie was over, I pushed open the heavy double doors into a cascade of thick salty raindrops. They were falling at a slant. Since my sweatshirt had a hood, I automatically pulled it up.

I jaywalked to the island where a trolley was parked. Depositing exact change, I chose one of four single seats. Riding by myself has always struck me as princely.

Privately congratulating myself for at least not having to spill my wetness onto another passenger, I gazed out the window. A triple image immediately came to view: myself as in a mirror, superimposed on the advertisements across the aisle, superimposed on the street, in shadow now that the rain had started.

Pillar Four:
Enriching and Refining

When you review your draft, you may be surprised at how bare the skeleton is. Flesh it out, sentence by sentence, paragraph by paragraph, so that it will not only make sense to another reader, but will more closely approximate your own intention. Sometimes this means reorganizing the whole project around a small transition that suddenly emerges as the central theme.

In our example, the writer might realize that she fully enters her subject with the sentence, "But when the movie was over. . . ." That is the beginning of her relationship with the rain and the interior state that this relationship nurtures. The part about walking to the theater when it was still sunny is irrelevant. However, identifying what her subject isn't makes it clearer what it is. Now she needs to deepen and intensify that subject.

When the movie was over, I pushed open the heavy double doors into a cascade of thick salty raindrops. They were falling at a slant, lifted by the ocean breeze.

Since my sweatshirt had a hood, I automatically pulled it up, then jaywalked to the island where a trolley was waiting. Except for the driver it was empty.

I chose one of four single seats and gazed out the window. Under the bright lights of the trolley a triple image immediately came into view—myself as in a mirror, besodden and a little shivery, superimposed on the advertisements across the aisle, superimposed on the street, in shadow now that the rain had started. Pedestrians dashed about, holding their belongings in one hand and their newspaper-hats in the other. They were getting drenched with each new gust of wind.

Pillar Five: Rest Periods

In writing, as in life, rest fosters growth. To allow your work to ripen and achieve clarity, it needs rest. Revise your work once and, if necessary, set it aside for another period of time. Reread it again with renewed objectivity. Two rest periods are ideal. For complex projects, a dozen is not overdoing it.

Though it was sunny before the movie started, I pushed open the heavy double doors into a cascade of thick salty raindrops. They were falling at a slant. Lifted by the ocean breeze, they looked like they were drawn by a cartoonist.

Since my sweatshirt had a hood, I automatically pulled it up. I jaywalked to the island where a trolley was parked. Drivers would often wait, allowing passengers to board, while they read the newspaper. When I rapped on the door, it opened with a sigh. I had the whole car to myself.

I chose one of four single seats. Privately congratulating myself for at least not having to drip over another passenger, I propped my backpack on my knees and turned to face the window. Under the bright lights of the trolley a triple image came to view. I saw myself as in a mirror, besodden and a little shivery, superimposed on the double-seats and advertisements across the aisle, superimposed on the street, in shadow now that the rain had started. Pedestrians were dashing down the sidewalk wearing newspapers for hats. They held their belongings in one hand, their newspaper-hats in the other and clumsily made their way forward getting drenched with each new gust of wind. The rain, if anything, was falling more heavily.

Part III

THE LESSON OF LITTLE RED RIDING HOOD

Transform obstacles into tools to deepen and intensify your writing practice.

EXERCISE

Sneaking Up on Your Mind

Experiment with writing at times you ordinarily wouldn't:

- the moment you wake up
- the middle of the night
- when you are in a moving vehicle
- on breaks from class or your place of employment
- while bathing
- in the midst of an uninteresting meeting/ lecture/conference
- in line at the post office

Your perhaps wacky or even unintelligible jottings may nonetheless reveal aspects of your mind that heretofore have remained hidden. As you reread them, teeny bits, like shells on a beach, will pop up and strike you as beautiful.

TIGERS IN THE

LOWLAND

"It's up to you to choose the appropriate mandala for the way in which you want to develop . . . just like you choose shoes that fit your feet!" Lama Yeshe reminds us. Part of deliberately doing anything is creating an environment that supports it. Paramahansa Yogananda is emphatic: "Environment is stronger than will." You will not attain your goals until you surround yourself with people who are actively striving toward similar ones.

Thich Nhat Hanh, yet another spiritual master, calls this principle "sangha (community) building:"

Sangha building is so crucial. If you are without a sangha, you lose your practice very soon. In our tradition we say that without the sangha you are like a tiger that has left his mountain and gone to the lowland—he will be caught and killed by humans.

If you practice without sangha you are abandoning your practice.

On the last day of every retreat, therefore, Thich Nhat Hanh organizes "sangha-building sessions." He says if his students are surrounded by a sangha, when they leave, they have a *chance* to continue their practice. Otherwise, in just a few weeks or months, they will be carried away and no longer able to even talk about practice.

Taking care of your environment and the practice that your environment sustains creates a level of immersion which *in itself* can become an environment.

A snapshot accompanying an article entitled "Ultra Runners" features Dipali Cunningham receiving a blessing from her guru Sri Chinmoy upon winning the men's and women's 700-mile Ultimate Ultra, a trio of races in which participants run 1,300, 1,000 or 700 miles over a period of 18 or 19 days. The runners circle a one-mile loop set on Wards Island Park across from the East Harlem River and the Manhattan skyline. Like tigers who have never left their mountain, they run without pause, slowing to a brisk walk for meals and sleeping maybe three hours a night.

If you try to become a writer with your will alone,

you are likely to fail. You must use your heart *and* your will to create an inner environment of "prowling" intention and an outer environment that is harmonious with your goals and includes like-minded prowlers.

EXAMINING YOUR ENVIRONMENT

Examine your environment with the sharp thoughts of what does and does not support a writing practice. (By "environment" I mean anything that affects you—your space, your relationships, your clothing, your belongings, your health, your finances, your work, your thoughts, your daily schedule, and so forth.) As you hold writing at the forefront of your consciousness, your life increasingly will provide a context for that activity, not only containing but promoting and inspiring it.

Invisible practice refers to tasks that come to your attention primarily when you have neglected them—brushing your teeth, emptying the garbage, straightening your desk. If you don't straighten your desk, the omission will be obvious the moment you can't lay your hands on a critical piece of paper. If you do—well, clean is just your desk's original nature.

Writers' invisible practices pertain both to writing and to a myriad of behind-the-scene activities: reading, journal-keeping, trips to the office supply store, filing, indexing, switching things around. Sometimes it seems that writing is 60 percent organization, 40 percent writing, and 10 percent this and that.

What about your first two, three, or even five drafts? It's business-as-usual to take that long just to achieve clarity. Does the reader of the final copy know? No.

And usage? "The eloquence of her prandial conversations stirs him deeply." ("Prandial" pertains to a meal, especially lunch or dinner.) How long does it take to be so skillful that the *very* word (the one that has precision, subtlety, depth, nuance) rolls off the tip of your pen? The French novelist Colette searched tirelessly for "the right word" and found it no less elusive after decades of writing.

Invisible practice. It helps to have a dignified name for what we might easily label ungratifying time-wasters.

THE GENTLE CYCLE

*The finest qualities of our nature, like the
bloom on fruits, can be preserved only by the
most delicate handling. Yet we do not treat
ourselves nor one another thus tenderly.*

— HENRY DAVID THOREAU

As a teenager, Anne Sexton remembers, "I read nothing but Sara Teasdale. I might have read other poets,
but my mother said as I graduated from high school
that I had plagiarized Sara Teasdale. Something
about that statement of hers . . . I had been writing
a poem a day for three months, but when she said
that, I stopped."

Unfortunately, the desire to write is more fragile than the desire by family, friends, and well-
intentioned others to prematurely extinguish it. All
too many a young writer's dreams have been quashed
by a single inept remark.

When it comes to feedback, why not treat yourself as you would a new piece of fine lingerie? At first you might wash it by hand or else on a machine's gentlest cycle with the mildest detergent. You might simply let your garment soak, not agitate it at all. Later, when you've experimented a few times and you know what it can handle, you might try tumbling it around. Eventually you might throw it in with the rest of your wash. But not before you are certain that its seams are strong, its dye won't fade and that the fabric can "take" rough treatment. Well, you (vis-a-vis your writing) deserve at least the same consideration.

Being emotionally and psychologically ready to re-ceive feedback presupposes an ability to use the feed-back constructively. "Constructively" means that you have achieved enough distance from your writing to understand, for instance, that "not quite" describes your paragraph, not you.

Let's say the feedback is negative. If someone crit-icizes your writing, your job is to listen. When the person is finished you thank them, then reflect on the truth of what you have heard. If you find that it is true, change your writing for the better. If you find that it is false, never consider it further. You win regardless because if you respond to criticism in this manner, there's little chance that you won't learn something about both yourself and your writing.

When a writer begins working on something, she herself may only have an inkling about its direction. That inkling (sprout) must be kept covered, sprinkled lightly with water, protected from wind and rain and in general allowed to grow and gather strength undisturbed by outside influences. Not until it is strong enough can it withstand the "other's" voice. Part of a writer's task is to learn to correctly gauge her own, and her writing's, readiness.

FEEDBACK:
A TOUCHY SUBJECT

There are three requirements for feedback to be effective: First, the writer must be emotionally and psychologically ready to receive feedback, i.e., she must be open to learning. Second, the person *giving* feedback must be (a) knowledgeable about the kind of writing being done by the writer, (b) knowledgeable about *how* to convey his evaluative information (giving feedback is a developed skill), and (c) he must *care* about this particular writer's writing. (Without caring he is likely to be out of tune with the writer, and his criticism, though perhaps accurate "by the book," may be off "by the heart.") Third, no matter how astute the feedback, if it is ill-timed, it will be useless, possibly even harmful.

Too often beginning writers turn to friends or family (people whom they like and trust on a personal level) for feedback on their writing. Family and friends are the *very ones* with the greatest power to shame. It is painful to see a talented student seeking feedback from a relative or friend who, in the name of being "supportive," encourages her in a direction that is unsuited to her strengths. Even worse is that the family member or friend may read old scripts "into" the writing or may fail to recognize the writer's real voice. Unless your friends and family are explicitly interested in and knowledgeable about the kind of writing you are doing, and are skilled in offering feedback, it is advisable to wait to share your writing with them. Instead, seek out someone who meets the three above "feedback giver" criteria.

WRITER'S BLOCK:

THE MAGIC MOUNTAIN

"Writer's block." A weighty, mule-like phrase. Perhaps such tonnage is needed to carry conviction. "Writer's block" indeed! There's no such thing.

"What!" cries one student, a brilliant man whose pen will produce nothing but clichés. "What!" cries another who out of shame, has stopped even trying to write. "You don't know how frustrating it is, day after day, to feel stymied."

For me the term "writer's block" conjures up the image of a road with a gigantic boulder across it. The boulder, bordered on one side by a cliff and on the other a lake, stops the traveler dead in his tracks.

His tendency, of course, is to wonder: (a) How could it (the boulder) have gotten there, (b) Can I lug it away, and (c) Can I get around or over it? All of these questions feature the boulder.

The boulder, however, is not the problem. The problem lies in the traveler's perspective—seeing the boulder as an obstacle instead of as a path. The boulder, a material manifestation of mind and spirit, contains the next step in his development. He must isolate its components, examine each microscopically, and integrate it with the person he becomes as a result of this process. There *are* tons of material.

Behind any "I won't" stance ("I won't eat." "I won't talk." "I won't budge.") is a loud scream. "Writer's block" blocks a deafening roar that perhaps even the screamer is afraid to hear. What's of interest is the roar, not what stifles it. When we focus on the "block" (that heavy-duty term has a way of commanding our attention), we get waylaid.

There is no such thing as "writer's block." Rather there are various forms of distraction. Do not look at your garden and say, "There are so many weeds in it I can't see the flowers. I guess I don't have a green thumb. Oh well." If there are so many weeds, look at the weeds. Dig them up, compost them, fertilize the flowerbed with your homemade compost, sow the seeds of your desires and keep weeding, composting, fertilizing, sowing—and watch your garden grow.

WRITER'S ANOREXIA:[16]

THE ABUSE OF

CREATIVE POWER

"If the self is left incomplete it will continually pull at our attention," Kim Chernin, psychotherapist and writer, has noticed and this dynamic is particularly evident in an anorexic. A shadowy figure, an "internal saboteur,"[17] thrives (like a parasite) on her debilitated psyche.

Often a symptom is an attempt at cure. "Writer's anorexia" is another way to describe (and treat) "writer's block."

The writer with "writer's anorexia" is as much a victim as the sufferer from the eating disorder. The more frightened she becomes (of her crippling fear of inner emptiness), the more strident the saboteur's threat: "Writing may be all-important but *you* will *never be able to*." Seeming to prove him right, endless blank pages reflect her sense of mental, emotional and spiritual vacuousness.

Her internal saboteur constantly affirms how stupid, untalented and uncreative she is. She is sure he is telling her the truth. Psychologically hypnotized, the person with "writer's anorexia" is completely convinced that she "can't" write. Of course the well-being of her saboteur depends on her remaining convinced.

As with all other problems based in the unconscious, the solution lies in awareness. An internal saboteur, pernicious in the dark, loses his power in the light of truth (and the individuation that results from truth).

Language can be the switch. The writer suffering from writer's anorexia must stay present to herself, mercilessly honest and *verbal* about her apparent inabilities. Soon, ensconced in words, "I feast, *you* fast" becomes *her* gig (as opposed to his).

GUIDELINES

The abuse of creative power paralyzes the mind so that the writer is no longer free to direct his or her psychic energy. To maintain a sense of self-coherence, those affected might benefit from the following guidelines:

1. Since women are enculturated to equate value with looks, women may be more self-conscious than men about the looks of their writing. A writer who cannot risk appearing "ugly," gives her power as a writer away to an interior version of the "fashion" industry. Just as it is demoralizing to be valued primarily as a body, it is likewise demoralizing (humiliating and deeply unsatisfying) to have one's writing valued primarily as an object-that-sells.

2. Women sometimes get raped because they have been taught not to heed their instincts (for danger, for example) and to "not make waves." Forthright is beautiful. Avoid becoming victim to your lesser talents.

3. Learn to distinguish between passion and addiction. The former enriches. The latter depletes.

4. Though will is important, for a writer, love is equally important. Never treat yourself like a drill sergeant.

5. Keep your life as simple as possible. What gets lost in the shuffle of chaos and confusion is *you.*

6. Find a succinct way to explain your writing

to curious "strangers." Awkward questions at awkward times can derail you and trigger a voice of self-doubt. (W.H. Auden was wont to tell people he didn't know that he was a "medieval historian.")

7. A writer's experience is a writer's material. No one can take it away from you. First write it. Trust that if you write your truth fully and conscientiously, you will make the correct decision about how to disperse what you have written. It could be that the child you thought you were protecting with silence will grow up and write about *you*.

8. Not being able to write is only one indicator of writer's anorexia. Another more insidious indicator is the production of imitative writing. This kind of writing feels weak even to the author and spins her into bouts of uncertainty. The solution: unwavering personal honesty. Perhaps no obstacle is greater to the flow of genuinely original writing than the tyranny of the false self. Whereas unacknowledged truth saps your resources, acknowledged truth replenishes the reserves.

9. Speaking directly to a shadowy internal oppressor is not easy. Do not be ashamed to ask for help. Unconscious secrets are most easily unlocked in the presence of a forgiving other.

THE LESSON OF

LITTLE RED

RIDING HOOD

After many years of struggle, a young man I know finally found a way to incorporate writing in his life on a regular basis. Even so, as soon as he gets discouraged, a voice inside his head starts up with the old "Why are you wasting your time doing this?" even though he *knows absolutely* that writing has helped (perhaps more than anything else) to organize his life and to make it meaningful. Inevitably, with the advent of the painfully familiar question, he gets depressed. Indeed, this voice is *very* persuasive and it *feels* unanswerable.

One of the reasons that it's so persuasive is that it is old. He has heard it a million times, probably from people he admires and respects and probably when he didn't have the life experience to question its validity. When a significant adult warns us that a prospective endeavor will lead nowhere, even if we are rebelling, a part of us pays close attention—with the result that we either avoid the endeavor and feel empty, or we do the endeavor anyway and feel guilty. Fresh wounds are painful, but repeated wounds are excruciating.

The solution? We need to learn to name the voice who is speaking to us and consciously decide how much power we want to give it. Like Little Red Riding Hood confronting the wolf who is dressed as her grandmother—"Why grandmother, what big eyes you have!"—the voice you hear in your moment of discouragement is not your grandmother's voice (the deeply empathic voice of someone who wants nothing more that your true happiness). It is the wolf's voice (your emotional and spiritual enemy). Far from the friendly voice of one ready to support you through time after difficult time, it is the voice of a powerful inner critic poised to prey upon your insecurity and guilt.

The voice does not require answering. Naming is enough. The moment you hear this voice, you must identify precisely who it is—a voice that is dedicated to undermining your newly-achieved (and bravely fought for) commitment to write. Once you identify the critic, its power will shrivel before your eyes.

Don't forget, Little Red Riding Hood *gave* the wolf (who relied on her innocence) all the power it had. If she knew who she was addressing, he wouldn't have gotten to first base.

IF WRITING IS YOUR PRACTICE, THE ONLY WAY TO FAIL IS TO NOT WRITE

Erroneous indicators of failure often have the devastating effect of inducing a real failure.

- I want to write but I don't feel driven. I don't *feel* "no matter what." Actually some days I do, but other days I feel quite lazy.
- For me, the longing to publish is so old and so deep that I can't get around it. It's like a sore. Only one balm will heal it.
- I write every morning but I like it best when I get a "buzz." If I sit there and nothing comes, I get impatient.
- I know I'm a good writer but I haven't found my "form." Without it I feel I don't know what I'm doing. Somehow writing doesn't "belong" to me.

- I definitely have writing skills but I can't get myself to finish anything.
- I keep being pulled away from my "own" writing by the thought "If I could write a screenplay and sell it, then I would have all the time in the world for my own writing."
- Sometimes I feel I'm just writing the same thing over and over. What's the point?
- Writing is really hard for me. Getting to the first draft is hard and it's impossible to imagine my pitiful language ever turning into the fine prose I see in the bookstores.
- I'm thirty-five. Many famous writers reached their peak in their adolescence or their twenties. Aren't I too old to just be starting out?
- I can't seem to get past "me." All my writing is about myself and renditions of my life. Even I'm bored with it.
- I long to write but I'm so afraid of failing (I fail at everything I try) that I can't bear to begin. I can't bear to fail at something I want this much.

All of the above are focused on *what*. The antidote: stay with *how*. If you emphasize the product, you are selling yourself short. Don't permit your self-esteem to rest on such flimsy bedding. Products have a shelf-life.

But *you* don't. Your soul is boundless. When you emphasize the process, your writing roams. The cosmos itself becomes your sitting room, your pen, the moon—around which, like stars, "problems" settle themselves.

"Writing parents!" Who ever heard of that? Well, children of writing need writing parents.

Writing parents must be tender, enthusiastic, extremely interested, humorous, nurturing, visionary, and knowledgeable. There needs to be someone further along the path than you to say "go!" Otherwise you crumple in your own lack of confidence.

One writer I know did not pick any writing parents. She is a writing orphan. "When I try to write creatively, I freeze," she says. "All I can think of is *this* time I probably won't excel." Her fear is not surprising. She had no mirroring and no "play space" to come into her own as a writer. Her inner command to perform is paramount.

Contrast this person's story with another writer who found a "writing mother." Her writing mother noticed everything, was sensitive to everything. She praised and laughed and delighted in unexpected turns of phrase. This writer "grew up" writing-wise in her writing mother's tremendously supportive presence.

Her "writing father" worked in a bookshop. She'd go there for hours and browse. Often he would read her his poems. Sometimes he'd leave a whole section of a poem-in-progress on her answering machine. He also gave her feedback on her writing.

During the years of meeting with her writing parents, her poetic voice was forming. It was unruly, subversive, erotic, extreme. She'd get afraid. "Who gave me permission to write like this?" She'd panic. "How do I know it's okay?" Wanting to die of embarrassment she'd meet her writing father and *he* gave her permission. *His* seeing what she was doing, appreciating and validating it, made it possible for her to continue.

Like waves, a rhythm develops . . . receiving support and validation from other people and returning to the ground of your own being. With each return you are a little bit stronger.

Part IV

BEAUTY

PLUS PITY

Our language is formed in turn by the pantry and the gate, by the rose and the lily, the dog and the fish and the tiger, the clouds and the stones. There is no language that is not the wording of our habitat, and no self whatever, except a temporary formation of the total environment.

—ROBERT AITKEN-ROSHI[18]

Watching the Mind

a. Sit quietly and for ten minutes record every single thought that crosses your mind. You can record each thought separately as you initially think it or in a jumble intermingled with new thoughts arising and old ones falling away. Record even snippets, flickerings of half-thoughts, even if they seem wildly irrelevant, off-the-wall, or shameful.

b. Same as above only in addition include emotions, the heavier-laden thought processes.

c. Weave (a) and/or (b) into a very short story. (This requires providing a context for them.)

IF I THINK ABOUT MYSELF, DOES THAT MEAN I'M SELFISH?

When a writer starts writing, she may think that the important thing is to demonstrate that she can write well. Thus she is busy evaluating, on whatever basis, the quality of what she has produced. "That's wonderful!" is what she really wants to hear. Actually, a beginning writer is building up a context for her writing, a body of material that will allow her to identify her strengths and interests as a writer.

Also, she may have been told that thinking about herself, constantly referring back to her own experiences, is selfish. Without a context, a writer may feel vulnerable to the accusation, "You're so selfish," to the shame and fear that it may be true.

Here are some examples of the skills and proclivities that emerged over a period of months in the work of novice writers:

- Meaning-making. This writer featured ideas and structure. Her thoughts flowed logically off her pen with a beginning, middle and end.
- Story-telling. Over and over this writer pulled her listeners in to intrigue wrapped around an emotional core.
- Short lyrical passages. Like stones across a brook, this writer skipped from phrase to strongly provocative phrase.
- Energy in language. This writer focused on each word, its inherent breath, and mobility.
- Nuance. Unpeeling layer upon layer of subtlety in any random subject, this writer deepened the seemingly trivial.
- "Being-living." This writer had a genius for penetrating the ever-elusive now.

As with any other kind of development, we first begin to see ourselves through someone else's eyes, which is why a mentor is important and why the words "You're so selfish" are damaging. They are judgmental rather than empathic and fail to "see" into the heart of the "selfish" one, who will in turn have trouble seeing into her own, more than likely, unselfish heart.

If you are a writer, you must ferret out your authentic voice/style/form. Thinking about yourself is not only *not* selfish, it is the discipline which you strive to perfect.

WRITER-JOCK

Not just cutting the carrot took attention, but picking the knife up, putting the knife down, wiping the knife, cleaning the knife, sharpening the knife, storing the knife.

—ED ESPE BROWN

The way you take care of anything is the way you take care of everything. If you don't take care of your writing tools (your pen, notebook, eraser, stapler, tape), you may not bother to take care of yourself. But wherefore comes your writing?

Taking care of your body is like sharpening a pencil. If you sharpen your pencil regularly, it will work well and you will probably not notice it much. (Pencil-sharpening is "invisible practice.") If you do not sharpen your pencil, gradually it will lose its edge; your hand-writing will be legible but smeared —not crisp—and finally, no writing will appear at all (the pencil stops working, shuts down). Your body is the same.

That may be why writers so often prepare for writing with a wordless, rhythmical, monotonous activity that grounds them in their bodies, absorbing outer attention while freeing inner. The author, Jack Kerouac, says that writing, like meditation and self-realization, is an athletic, physical accomplishment.

Though you may resent your body and all its needs, body intelligence is a kind of consciousness just like any other kind of consciousness.

It is impossible to separate the mind from the body and spirit. The part that lags behind will glare from the written page. Human language derives from the physical nature of man. "It was the nerves and not the intellect which created speech."[19]

WRITING AND "RIGHT" LIVELIHOOD

> Paris Review: *Do you think that the optimal career for a poet would involve no work at all but writing and reading?*
>
> *T.S. Eliot: I think that for me it's been very useful to exercise other activities, such as working in a bank, or publishing . . . the difficulty of not having as much time as I would like has given me greater pressure of concentration.*

The crucial "right" livelihood issue (for a writer) pertains not so much to *what* she does (teaching, working at the post office, selling insurance) as to the quality of the state of mind she is able to cultivate while she does it. Indeed, the term "right," as Robert Aitken-roshi explains in his book *The Original Dwelling Place*, should be understood to mean "in accord with the essentially vacant, interdependent, and richly varied nature of things."

At bottom, "right" livelihood is a practical matter. One simply cannot be in a foul state of mind for part of the day and expect to arrive at her writing period in a pristine one. Remember, writers are always writing whether they are writing or not. Choosing a job that supports one's intention to write is simply part of creating the "right" environment for one's writing.

While most writers understandably dream of making their living practicing their craft, there are (as T.S. Eliot indicates) advantages to making your living in other ways:

- They might broaden your range of skills.
- They may expand your sources of inspiration.
- By enlarging your experience, these other ways might contribute both to your strength of character and your compassionate understanding of other people's suffering.
- Deadlines will be your deadlines, subjects your subjects. Your writing will be done at your speed, directed by your heart.
- By having only one "boss" (you), your writing will have more privacy/autonomy.

- By striving to achieve *your* vision, your writing may have greater purity/integrity.
- The fulfillment of your basic needs will not be jeopardized by the state of disenfranchisement of writers.
- The fact that you earn your living in ways other than "your" writing may make "your" writing all the more yours.

WHO IS WRITING

BETTER VEDAS?

"Look what I found in the grass!" cries a five-year-old running through a field of wildflowers. What is remarkable is not what he found, but his enthusiasm, which has transformed a marble into a sparkling, magical conveyer of light. Enthusiasm, like the breath of God, transforms everything.

> If only we refuse to take our world for granted, we can detect something artful lurking at the heart of life, inviting us deeper into the world, allowing us to penetrate further and further into the mystery of its creation, perhaps even promising us a new relation to everything we know.[20]

At first this new relation concerns perception—as if suddenly we were presented with a pair of astonishing lenses. Later the focus turns to discipline.

Rightfully (since the one ignites the other), discipline and enthusiasm will be close friends.

Thoreau wrote every day. He kept a journal (the place in which he made "a huge effort to expose [his] innermost and richest wares to light"), a notebook for recording passages from his reading, and, in addition, a set of notebooks for recopying the distilled essence of his earlier ones (which amounted to hundreds of pages). After all this writing, he concluded: "A perfectly healthy sentence is extremely rare."

But he was willing to work hard and to be judged by the result.

While good writing is difficult to produce, without enthusiasm, "difficult" becomes "impossible."

And *with* enthusiasm? Thoreau asked of himself (as if to make it a personal requirement), "Who is writing better Vedas?"

RIPPLES ON THE SURFACE OF THE WATER

The fatal flaw . . . is his regarding (recurrent words, such as "garden" or "water") as abstractions, and not realizing that the sound of a bath being filled, say, in the world of Laughter in the Dark, *is as different from the limes rustling in the rain of* Speak, Memory *as the Garden of Delights in* Ada *is from the lawns of* Lolita.[21]

Just as a scene captured by a photographer is not so much about the scene as it is about the vision and perspective of the photographer, so it is with "scenes" captured by writers. Consider the following description of a woman's beauty by nineteenth-century novelist George Eliot:

It is the beauty like that of kittens, or very small downy ducks making gentle rippling noises with their soft bills, or babies just beginning to toddle and engage in conscious mischief—a beauty with which you can never be angry, but that you feel ready to crush for inability to comprehend the state of mind into which it throws you.

While writers through the millennium have tried to depict the mysterious beauty of women, George Eliot's lens is peering not at beauty *per se* so much as the hapless state of mind that it evokes. Her concern is not with kittens but with the loss of judgment and control admirers suffer in the face of their beguiling sweetness.

In *No Nature* (its last poem) Gary Snyder notices "Ripples on the surface of the water/ were silver salmon passing under—different/from the ripples caused by breezes. . . ." and suddenly we are aware of ripples, those made by a swimming fish, by a breathing fish, by a boy fishing, by the autumn wind, by ducks, by a plunging stone, by a canoe of lovers, by a youngster's sailboat. We are aware of the surface of the water being absolutely still before being disturbed and then gradually returning to stillness. We are aware of different textures of water—some sparkling clear, others strewn with mud and silt. We imagine the moon reflecting off one inky surface, the sun off another, insects swarming, inner-tubes floating. Snyder makes a single fine distinction and bam!—the water is alive to us in a million possible renditions.

Objects are filled with information, saturated with power. Careful observation unleashes this power, which gushes forth effusively. Sealed in the spawning silver salmon are all the projections, associations, illusions, fantasies, memories, stories, dreams that we have ever concocted around rivers and salmon season and eating salmon and who we were with while we were eating salmon. And *their* ripple effect—Huckleberry Finn, Aunt Sally, Miss Watson and runaway Jim. It is as difficult to distinguish between a river and a ripple in the river as it is between a salmon and our soul infusing it with life.

ART IS THEFT,

ART IS ARMED ROBBERY,

ART IS NOT PLEASING

YOUR MOTHER

A minor poet borrows, a great poet steals, T.S. Eliot said implying that borrowing is a form of appropriation whereas stealing affects a change so fundamental that the object stolen loses its original nature. Actually, it is impossible to steal language.

It is impossible to steal language because of our inherent individuality and unique relationship with words. The same word from my pen is different from that from yours because the word has for me a personal derivation (I discovered it under unrepeatable circumstances), a personal history (I have integrated it into my autobiography in relation to which it has its own urgency), a personal aura (both its derivation and history color my feelings toward it and the way

I interact with it) and a place in my personal lexicon (unlike the lexicon of another living being).

Regarding language, "taking" = "borrowing with the intent to transform" even if that "intent" is unconscious. (And a good thing too or our English wouldn't be half as rich.) Alchemy, not thievery is at issue. An English word "taken" from the German retains its German flavor. A quotidian word of yours, elixir-like, beams its golden spell across my text.

Words are not rabbits. A skilled magician can put a rabbit under a hat and poof!, it's gone . . . (much applause). If a skilled poet (magician of language) puts your word under her hat, it will come out hers because of her intrinsic creative relationship with that word.

Derivative writers seem versatile because they imitate many others, past and present. Artistic originality has only its own self to copy.

Which is why "artistic originality" is so magical.

Introducing a radically innovative paper to the British Psychoanalytical Society, D.W. Winnicott refused to trace his ideas back to other people's theories:

. . . My mind does not work that way. What happens is that I gather this and that, here and there, settle down to clinical experience, form my own theories, and then, last of all, interest myself to see where I stole what.[22]

Nevermind where a poet gets his words. People take what they feel is rightfully theirs and pay for it with respect. The pointing fingers of lesser talent aside, in the world of writing, words of pure intent are unencroachable.

"Virtue is beauty is one's essential nature," Suzuki-roshi once told a disciple. By trying to write something beautiful, you may be superimposing a preconceived notion (with an inherent value judgment) on the natural rhythm of your expression. But embedded in the notion of beauty is authenticity. It doesn't allow for the superimposition of anything. Writers, painters, and other Zen masters have defined beauty similarly:

Gary Snyder: ". . . For language to do its job—articulate the nature of reality—it must be intricate, nonsymmetrical, chaotic."

Gertrude Stein (paraphrasing Picasso in defense of his early cubist paintings): ". . . The inventor because he does not know what he is going to invent inevitably the thing he makes must have its ugliness."

Ralph Waldo Emerson (in explanation of his famous line "Beauty is its own excuse for being"): "Beauty is primary, basic, foundational, a given." It is not a secondary attribute or a means of praising something we really prefer for other reasons.

Soen-roshi: "Beauty is unrepeatable."

Virginia Woolf: ". . . there is a risky connection between originality and incoherence."

Kazuo Ishiguro's protagonist in *An Artist of the Floating World* comments on the transitory, illusory quality of geisha and their environments: "The finest, most fragile beauty an artist can hope to capture drifts within those pleasure houses after dark."

Vladimir Nabokov: "*Beauty plus pity*—that is the closest we can get to a definition of art."

Beauty is a trap. The concept of beauty, not the thing itself. It's a waste of time to try to write beautiful writing.

A BUTTON AND
A FEW BONES

🌿

One ought to write carefully enough so that a piece would need at least three readings before its full beauty could be apprehended.
— HENRY DAVID THOREAU

In July 1850, Ralph Waldo Emerson's good friend, the writer and transcendentalist Margaret Fuller, was returning to America from Italy with her husband and infant son when her ship struck an offshore sandbar five miles east of Fire Island. Only the captain's wife, the acting captain and a few of the crew survived. Henry David Thoreau, as Emerson's emissary, joined the thousands of scavengers to pilfer through floating debris to obtain information, manuscript fragments and other property of Margaret's.

When Bayard Taylor, a *Tribune* reporter, described the scene, he emphasized the sea, the wreck, the efforts of the insurers to reach and survey the damage, the cargo, the general litter of the beach, as well as the crowds of people thronging to see this vast public calamity.

Thoreau's account was entirely different. In his wandering about the shallows, he had found a coat of Margaret's husband's from which he removed a button. Thoreau also saw a portion of a human skeleton. *This* is what he wrote about. "By focusing on the button and the few bones, he remove[d] the entire public scene, creating a feeling of being alone, lost in the middle of a great empty space."[23]

Thoreau was writing "down." Writing "down" means to plunge into the depth of a detail, extract its essence and allow this to permeate and vitalize the piece as a whole. Writing "down" makes the minutia of an imaginary world spring to life.

An alert mind relishes every shade of gray and manipulates its distinctive personality to serve its own agenda. For example, metaphor and simile bring subtlety, intricacy and profundity to one's language. "The unpretending truth of a simile implies sometimes such distinctness in the conception as only experience could have supplied,"[24] which makes the writing vivid and personal.

Writers must sink into the interior life of things,

of people, of events, of relationships. You need to swim the whole ocean, but to grasp its essential nature you need to pause, rest on a sandbar and watch the playfulness of the fish, the undercurrents in the sand or the fronds waving in a kelp forest. "No one sees further into a generalization than his own knowledge of details extends," Thoreau insisted. No wonder that in their habit of close attention, every poet has trembled on the verge of science.

Zen Master Dogen said, "Life is not killed." It is infinite and unbounded, though it changes and as part of that change, death happens. Reb Anderson (a Zen priest) explains: "Life does not die . . . Life is just life-ing, and then it is gone."

On the wings of art, might we sail beyond the prison-isle of time? Henry James' vessel was composed of endless, intricately entangled sentences; Jane Austen's, of seamlessly gliding lines. James Joyce melded together bits and pieces of the unconscious while Virginia Woolf's skillful hands turned a "terrific whiff of the past" into a rock-solid raft.

". . . We don't have complete emotions about the present, only about the past,"[25] Virginia Woolf observed. Thoreau's essay "A Winter Walk" was composed in early summer. "The first sparrow of spring" (one of the most famous passages in *Walden*), was written as fall approached. Like William Wordsworth, Henry David Thoreau's "feelings recollected in tranquility" came linguistically to fruition when his inner season was right.

Skeptics object. Even if we capture all the dust and floating microbes (i.e., the erratic, improbable, fantastic, snippets of the unconscious), the act of writing includes the present (and the perspective of the present) which falsifies the past.

The truth: Though there may be an inflexible barrier between the self inside and the world outside, between the past and the present, language—in its ungraspable, incorrigible, unpindownable yet deeply personal nature can almost breach it. Within the "fable-ridden loom" of subjectivity, it catches a tenderness in the familiar that only posterity will discern.

Part V

❦

A WORD
IS A CHARGED
SITUATION

Proust so titillates my own desire for expression that I can hardly set out the sentence. Oh, if I could write like that! I cry. And at the moment such is the astonishing vibration and saturation and intensification that he procures—theres [sic] something sexual in it—that I feel I can write like that, and seize my pen and then I can't write like that. Scarcely anyone so stimulates the nerves of language in me: it becomes an obsession.

—VIRGINIA WOOLF [26]

❦

Mot Juste

Ralph Waldo Emerson felt that each situation has its "right" word or precisely appropriate expression. Finding it involves more than cleverness because the truly right word comes from your large mind. You "immerse" your way into it.

For six weeks, write a haiku every day. This neatly circumscribed task induces the required concentration and presence, but any form of poetry will suffice, including poetic prose. A *mot juste* is a test. When your mental bell rings, it means you pass.

As I crawl over those rocks, I keep repeating, in a kind of zestful, copious, and deeply gratifying incantation, the English word "childhood," which . . . becomes stranger and stranger as it gets mixed up in my small, overstocked, hectic mind, with Robin Hood and Little Red Riding Hood, and the brown hoods of old hunchbacked fairies. There are dimples in the rocks, full of tepid water, and my magic muttering accompanies certain spells I am weaving over the tiny sapphire pools.

—VLADIMIR NABOKOV[27]

When the Russian novelist Vladimir Nabokov was a toddler, he announced to his mother that the colors of his alphabet blocks were wrong. "Well why dear?" Whereupon she learned that, like herself, he related colors to spoken sounds. To Elena Nabokov who appreciated symbolic connections, "Vladimir's crisp association of 'steely x, thundercloud z, and huckle-berry k' may have seemed a preparatory pastel sketch of the future artist as a young boy."[28]

Words are symbols and each one can evoke a singular response in the individual who hears it. To a six-year-old, for example, the term "guerrilla warfare" may conjure up a very frightening image dramatically different from the one likely to be in the mind of a thirty-year-old man. We all "own" words, even non-words. They are a part of our heritage. Making this ownership conscious can immensely enrich the relationship we establish with our language.

It could be, for example, that your companions never hear a certain word without thinking of the punch-line to a private joke. Or perhaps you have always felt sure of the meaning of a word—trapezoid—(and since you never looked it up, you took this meaning for granted) only to learn later about its geometric irregularities. Or maybe everyone in your family uses a certain non-word ("nother") on purpose. Or maybe to this day, a word that you learned studying invertebrates in seventh grade still trumpets through your brain as a bizarre concoction of sounds.

You might vividly recall learning a particular word and find that an irrelevant detail of your learning environment (chipped paint, cigarette butts) is still glued to it. Or perhaps you precociously learned a "big" word (ennui) that stays with you.

Consider the following:

> . . . one writes an address heaps of times, automatically and correctly, and then all of a sudden one hesitates, one looks at it consciously, and one sees you're not sure of it, it seems unfamiliar—very queer . . . You know, like taking a simple word, say "ceiling" and seeing it as "sealing" or "sea-ling" until it becomes completely strange and feral, something like "iceling" or "inglice."[29]

And afterwards (if this had happened to you) your relationship with the word "ceiling" would never regain its virginity.

". . . Language is fossil poetry." Words are fossil ethics and fossil history as well.
—RICHARD TRENCH, ORIGINATOR OF
THE OXFORD ENGLISH DICTIONARY

While Tibetan, for example, is capable of expressing the spiritual nature of reality with an exactitude for which English is entirely unequipped, there is far more depth, elasticity and subtlety in English than has been plumbed by its average user. It is painful to see ignorance and/or laziness whitewash the intricacies and delicate flavors with which our language is replete. By colluding, we give away a form of power. Most of us speak and write with our hands tied behind our backs.

Take the word "celibate." "Having taken up the practice of yoga, Jane decided to be celibate for a year." But "celibate" (its first definition) doesn't mean abstinence from sexual relations. It means to be unmarried, especially as a result of a religious vow. While the *second* definition of "celibate" *is* "abstention from sexual intercourse," to know that its first definition has to do both with a religious vow *and* being unmarried vastly enriches its ambience.

"Well so?" you might ask. "Who really cares? We knew what Jane meant. Why make picayune distinctions?"

A writer in part derives her power from so-called "picayune" distinctions. Because they aren't picayune. (Picayune means insignificant. Originally it referred to a coin of small value.) Rather they are *correct but small* differences in meaning that skillful hands can turn to *great* significance.

Take the word "cuirass"—a close-fitting armor for protecting the breast or back. Though at first glance you might label it archaic and get on with the dishes, Nabakov's "starched shirtfront swelling cuirasslike out of his waistcoat" will swing your head back around with a gasp.

Or "haruspication"—to inspect the entrails of animals and foretell future events therefrom. "Yuk!" you might say. "I'd never use such a word." But an essay criticizing overly analytical women, who, the author contends, practice "emotional haruspication" might revise your opinion.

Or "flocculence" which means "woolly or fluffy."
"Two flocculent beds . . ." Can't you picture them?

Gertrude Stein used to get irritated at her partner
Alice's predictable attraction to a certain type of
woman. So she introduced her to a friend wishing,
she said, to provide Alice with something less meretricious to worship. "Meretricious" means falsely at-
tractive/having the character of a prostitute. The one
(well-chosen) word tells the whole story.

"Nullifidian." Pink-polyestered nullifidians swarm
the church plaza. A nullifidian is a person without
depth or religious faith.

Consider her "farrago" of platitudes . . . farrago
means medley, mixture or hotchpotch. Or "backfisch" foolery . . . backfisch refers to a girl in late
adolescence. Or "caracoles" the waves of the sunny
ocean . . . caracole is a spiraling or turning to the
right and left alternately. Or the mountain glistened,
mirrored in the "coruscations" of her eyes . . . to
coruscate means to sparkle or glitter. Don't you wish
you had one of these for every occasion?

THE TOLD STORY

It took a long time to explain the fragility and intricacy because no word exists alone, and the reason for choosing each word had to be explained with a story about why it must be said this certain way. That was the responsibility that went with being human, old Ku'oosh said, the story behind each word must be told so there could be no mistake in the meaning of what had been said; and this demanded great patience and love.

—FROM AN UNKNOWN NATIVE AMERICAN CEREMONY

Children listen to the same story, with the same pleasure, perhaps even increased pleasure, with the thousandth retelling. The knowledge that in the end Goldilocks lives happily ever after decreases their fear not one iota when she is confronted with Papa Bear, Mama Bear and even little Baby Bear. At each beginning there is the same dread. When it is over, they sigh with the same relief. The partial trance into which they fall, while safely suspended in a fantasy, rocks them to sleep.

A story cradles the psyche. Listening becomes a form of embrace. The French word *recit* ("the told story") carries a sense of the narrator's soothing voice.

An old Zen tale illustrates this point. Near dusk an itinerant storyteller is passing through a village when he notices the *dojo* of a samurai. In the process of requesting lodging, he challenges the sword-master to a duel. At dawn they face off. The storyteller begins, "Long ago, in a village far away . . ." "Stop!" cries the sword-master bowing to his opponent. "The storyteller has won. I was transported by his words and could have been killed in an instant."

When we initially hear a story, we not infrequently attribute to it interest which belongs to our own untold sequel. We race to fill in the blanks. If its lines are overly crowded, no space is left for us to emboss the tale with our own intelligence.

We are all, despite ourselves, drenched in narrative. Implicit in every syllable of our uninterrupted inner monologue is testimony to an entire life. Retelling it (like prayer) becomes a way of relinquishing, a way of overcoming. Since we constantly reimagine ourselves in this fashion, we need to learn to self-listen with a child's rapt attention. Certainly we are as deserving of it as of Goldilocks.

ART FOR

LIFE'S SAKE

The rhythm of walking gets into her [Virginia Woolf's] sentences, the phrases she thinks of while looking and walking are saved and used.[30]

Have you ever been in a hurry and found yourself behind a sluggish driver on a single-lane street? That's cadence (a maddeningly slow one). For a writer, cadence is the balanced rhythmic flow of her voice, which mirrors the texture of her consciousness. A meandering page-long Henry James sentence, for example, replicates the almost imperceptible way the intricacies of our interior life gradually dawn on us. Gertrude Stein's repetitions depict her experience of layered, staccato-like heuristic revelations. It would be impossible, without some degree of falsification, to extricate either of their philosophies from the cadence with which they have chosen to express it.

Like diction and prosody, a writer's cadence is unique. Rarely left to chance, writers work hard to insure that their cadence, consistent with their intent, reflects "consciousness at full stretch."

Writing is like breathing, done everyday, by (practically) everyone on the planet. But when you deepen your writing practice—when your voice becomes "your" voice—your words will sing; not the jingle that we all recognize from grammar school—the one whose phonemes never quite made it to a full-fledged word. But the one, preeminently unpackagable, created even as your throat howls high above the treetops, quickening, teetering on the threshold of the heretofore unimagined "art for life's sake."

CADENCES

Here are some examples of characteristically cadenced writing by well-known writers. (For the curious, their names are provided in the endnotes.)[31]

1. "Polly was a slim girl of nineteen; she had light soft hair and a small full mouth. Her eyes,

which were grey with a shade of green through them, had a habit of glancing upwards when she spoke with anyone, which made her look like a little perverse madonna."

2. "Jeanne d'Arc worked a plough like a man; she wasn't a mimsy thing like Possy Luke with her cracked spectacles."

3. "Three girls, all fair, came down the cliff-side arm in arm, dressed in short, white trousers. Their arms and legs and throats were brown as berries; I could see when they laughed that their teeth were very white; they stepped on to the beach, and Brazell and Skully stopped singing. Sidney smoothed his hair back, rose casually, put his hands in his pockets, and walked towards the girls, who now stood close together, gold and brown, admiring the sunset with little attention, patting their scarves, turning smiles on each other. He stood in front of them, grinned, and saluted: 'Hullo, Gwyneth! do you remember me?' "

4. ". . . Not as oneself did one find rest ever."

5. "And yet it all came back, the taste of it, the tang and brine of it, like the windy crispy newspaper afternoon air over the san francisco wharves."

6. "The street and the marketplace absolutely

babbled, from side to side, with applause of the minister."

7. "The last rains lifted the corn quickly and scattered weed colonies and grass along the sides of the roads so that the gray country and the dark red country began to disappear under a green cover."

8. "His first consciousness was a sense of the light dry wind blowing in through the windows, with the scent of hot sun and sagebrush and sweet clover; a wind that made one's body feel light and one's heart cry 'Today, today,' like a child's. . . ."

THE LOOK OF
A VOICE

*Real verse music is not the melody of the verse.
Authentic verse music is that mystery which
brims over the rational texture of the line.*[32]

Samuel Taylor Coleridge noticed that art grows or-
ganically like a pear on its branch, not like a bowl
on a potter's wheel. For writing to be organic, its
form must allow the exigencies of content to bulge
and burst like a "sponge-bag containing a small fu-
rious devil."

Consider Mabel Dodge's description of her friend
Gertrude Stein's writing method:

> . . . She suspends her selective faculty, waiting for
> the word or group of words that will perfectly inter-
> pret her meaning, to rise from her sub-consciousness
> to the surface of her mind. . . . She does not go

after words—she waits and lets them come to her
. . . and they do. . . .[33]

"The human mind writes what it is," Gertrude
Stein said.

"Creating is not remembering but experiencing. . . .
It is to look and to hear and to write—without remembering. It is the immediate feelings arranged in
words as they occur to me."[34]

To awaken to words—to their aura, color, temperature, vibrancy, speed, weight, bulk, valence—we
must awaken to ourselves. Ernest Hemingway said if
a writer knows something, it will be present in his
language even if it is absent in his subject. Often a
writer's skill is commensurate with his ability to be
aware of what is present, to push it as far as it will
go. The cock crows when there is dawn *in me* and
my words alarm the universe.

Words convey sounds. "Thunderstorm,"
"thrush," "bell," "croak"—each has its own tonality,
pitch, decibel, even part of speech. Thoreau, for example, "moved past the mere naming of trees—the
nouns of the forest—to track its verbs: the birds, ro-
dents, and insects that pollinate flowers. . . ."[35]

Sounds fulfill similar duties. As one wafts into our consciousness, it must join and influence the particular set of biases, cumulative history and momentary state of harmony or discord that it finds there.

The recently revealed Kototama principle (Kototama means "word soul")[36], a tradition previously secreted by the Japanese royal family, affirms this.

> According to the Kototama, the sounds are the most central essences, to which trigrams of the *I Ching,* numbers, elements, color, etc., are related. The sounds contain all the essential possibilities and thus together form a complete matrix or "mirror" for reflecting almost any content. These sounds are the basis for building words regardless of the specific language.

That language "speaks" a meta-language of its own is infinitely apparent to Hikari (Kenzaburo Oë's mentally disabled son, a composer). The important thing is not so much the content but the musicality of human speech, or, as Hikari puts it, "the look of a voice." In daily conversation, when Hikari's syntax is unclear, he preserves throughout a sentence the same pattern of intonation. Through a sustained sound, the rapture of his meaning emerges. He requires neither sense nor syntax to release the voice of his wailing soul.

The written word also has a "look." Its "build" is alchemical, even as a woman's build. In its timbre (its mental ring) as well as its juxtaposition with other words, there is a resonance that can be squelched by speech. Though we may pronounce a word similarly, its silent sound is like "a white bird in snow." (Poets are sometimes loathe to read their poetry aloud, as if something precious will be lost sharing *that* version.)

Sorrow and pain, joy and ecstacy, wash through words. They need to breathe, to hike with the wind, to sail on clouds whose residual impression crosses our brow, catches us unawares, suddenly, with a jolt of realization.

GRASP THE THING,

WORDS WILL FOLLOW

> *The word Brahman is said to derive from the*
> *root* brh, *which means to swell or to grow. It*
> *signifies the rising of the word from the depths*
> *of the unconscious, the growth into con-*
> *sciousness.*[37]

While contemporary writers increasingly rejoice in the use of fragmented language, contemporary readers find it difficult to enter work they experience as abrasive (downright pushing them away). What do writers have to say that requires such jarring contextual extremes?

Heinz Kohut[38], a psychoanalyst who came to the United States from Vienna during World War II, was one of the first to attempt an answer. Modern artists, he said, in depicting the emotional, psychological and

spiritual problems of modern society, have an un-
precedentedly complex task:

> Just as it is the understimulated child, the insuffi-
> ciently responded-to child, the daughter deprived of
> an idealizable mother, the son deprived of an ideal-
> izable father, so it is the crumbling, decomposing,
> fragmenting, enfeebled self of this child and, later,
> the fragile, vulnerable, empty self of the adult that
> the great artists of the day describe. . . . and that
> they try to heal. The musician of disordered sound,
> *the poet of decomposed language,* the painter and
> sculptor of the fragmented visual and tactile world:
> they all portray the breakup of the self and through
> the reassemblage and rearrangement of the frag-
> ments, try to create new structures that possess
> wholeness. (emphasis added)[39]

Kohut moreover pointed out that while the art of
Henry Moore, Eugene O'Neill, Picasso, Stravinsky,
Pound, and Kafka would have been unintelligible
even a hundred years ago (he wrote this in 1977),
today, it is precisely *because* of their intricate and
nonsymmetrical order that we admire them.

Poetry is how language experiences itself [Gary Snyder tells us]. It's not that the deepest spiritual insights cannot be expressed in words (they can, in fact) but that *words* cannot be expressed in words. So our poems are full of *real presences.*

Which are untamable (and uncontainable). Language situates us in our life by perpetually instilling, drenching our experience with what is vigorous and free—loaded to the gills.

"Art, beauty and craft have always drawn on the self-organizing 'wild' side of language and mind," Gary Snyder claims, because "wild" is the way that phenomena continually actualize themselves. Our ability to tune into that wildness—with greater and greater accuracy to render it alive by portraying it in our self-reflections—ironically bespeaks of that very measure of health and wholeness the lack of which is of such concern. Our ability to stay present with the chaos may in the end be our salvation. Poets and artists (our generation's spokespeople) seem to think so.

❦

Some people misuse diamonds but that doesn't make diamonds any the less beautiful. Words are often misused. Sometimes words are used to "nail down" and deaden living things. The culprit is the person driving the hammer, not the hammer.

It's tricky. One person might learn the names of California flora, relish them, frolic through the genus and species of its entire binomial nomenclature. Another might learn the very same names and manage to reduce the world of wildflowers to a tiresome list. This doesn't make names bad. One's relationship with names, however, may need tending.

A word by its very nature has a kind of cohesion. It is autonomous yet stands for something else. Each word steeps within itself different infusions of the idea or object depicted (which is why it is useful to have more than one word for the same thing).

For a poet, a word is a charged situation. For this reason, Walt Whitman could say that a good poet "can make every word he speaks draw blood."

Here are some of the ways that a word can be violated:

1. Through overuse, a word grows limp and loses the electricity needed to generate a vivid image. (This slumber is what Gertrude Stein was fighting in her "Rose is a rose is a rose . . ." Unexpected repetitions woke her readers up.)

2. A word can be "dumbed down." It starts out with a million nuances and ends up, by popular demand, blatant—with no nuance whatsoever. For example, we use the word "gambit" to mean a ploy or tactic. Rightfully, and more subtly, it refers to an opening move that involves a strategic sacrifice or concession. All gambits are opening moves but not all opening moves are gambits, which, by the way, is why "opening gambit"—like "pizza pie"—is redundant.

3. A word can stand for too many situations/ideas and uphold none of them. Whenever it is used, listeners inadvertently make assumptions. Eventually even the assumptions are abandoned. Because no one takes the trouble to ascertain the word's original meaning, its "given" meaning, al-

beit vague, carries a general consensus. "Alibi" is an example. We use it to mean any excuse. But in legal parlance it refers to a plea by an accused person that she was elsewhere at the time she was alleged to have committed a crime. It carries a unique subtext of transferring responsibility.)

4. A word or phrase without heart (e.g., "all intents and purposes") is a dull dry thing.

5. A word can be used without its user earning the "right" to it. Thoreau wrote the following words when he was eleven. He had already earned the right. I know because when I read them, the precocity of his essential nature (he already knew how to leave distinctly Thoreau-ian space around his words; even his misspellings are touching) shines so brightly it makes me cry.

In Autumn we see the trees loaded with fruit. Now the farmers begin to lay in their Winter's store, and the markets abound with fruit. The trees are partly stripped of their leavs. The birds whith visited us in Spring are now retireing to warmer countries, as they know that Winter is coming.

Next comes Winter. Now we see the ground covered with snow, and the trees are bare. The cold is so intense that the rivers and brooks are frozen.

There is nothing to be seen. We have no birds to cheer us with their morning song. We hear only the sound of the sleigh bells.[41]

6. A word can be taken for profane ("bitch").

7. A word can be borrowed and mishandled (abused). "Aroma," of Greek origin, does not refer to just any smell, but only to pleasant ones.

8. A word (e.g., "arrogate"—a relative of "arrogance"—to assume without a right, or "noisome" which describes unpleasant smells, not noise) can get lost.

9. A word can suffocate rather than enlighten the listener. "Obsolescent" (things that are *becoming* obsolete), "perspicuity" (easily understood as "a perspicuous explanation"), "presumptive" (to give grounds to presume) are usually misused with the intention to impress.

10. A word can be constrained into an awkward position by archaic grammatical rules. *Woe Is I* (the title of a book on modern English usage) is a send-up of this very dilemma.

11. The opposite of No. 10—a word can be so rampantly misused in the vernacular that a layman

doesn't realize it. "Alot" (two words) is an example. Its original nature is squelched.

Would that there were "park rangers" of language who cited offenders and rewarded protec-
tors of our disappearing language. Where are the
conscientious objectors to the erosion of English?
"Wild by Law" must preserve words as zealously
as endangered animals.

Part VI

"NO, NO—
POETRY IS SERIOUS!
ZEN IS NOT SERIOUS."

Just before his teacher Oda Sesso-roshi died, Gary Snyder, having stopped writing for six years in order to be "serious" about Zen, said to his teacher in the hospital: "Roshi! So it's Zen is serious, poetry is not serious." The Roshi replied, "No, no—poetry is serious! Zen is not serious."

Silence Is Not Silence
Is Not Silence

Every silence has its signature tone, aura, energy field. Deepening one's relationship with silence, appreciating its nuances, is one way to practice the art of saturated writing.

a. Find a way to describe five different silences precisely.

b. Within each of five clamorous settings filter out the silent core and articulate its nature.

THE GOSPEL ACCORDING

TO THIS MOMENT

> *Looking back over the first 50 years of my*
> *career, I can find nothing that I have done*
> *that is worthwhile. At the age of 73 I have at*
> *last arrived at the point where I can perceive*
> *the true form and characteristics of birds, an-*
> *imals and plants. Thus my true life as an*
> *artist is just beginning.*
>
> —KATSUSHIKA HOKUSAI

Seeing is the crucial starting point for a writer. In fact without seeing, there is no writing. Seeing is the *way* that a writer writes.

Ordinary seeing, a quasi-conscious, semi-seeing, takes the world for granted. Without constant attentiveness to the unique, erratic, unpredictable particulars of our existence, seeing can decay into a rigidity of vision that diminishes and deadens us.

Practicing "deliberate seeing"—alert, aware, intelligent seeing—one develops reverence or the ability to see with the mind of a beginner. In his 1857 instructions to painters, art critic and theorist John Ruskin evokes the image of colors ". . . as a blind man would see them if suddenly gifted with sight."

Thoreau was intensely moved by Ruskin's description of a rose and copied it into his natural history notebook:

> The victorious beauty of the rose as compared with other flowers, depends wholly on the delicacy and quantity of its colour gradations, all other flowers being either less rich in gradations, not having so many folds of leaf; or less tender, being patched and veined instead of flushed.

Ruskin's receptivity, if not abandon, in the face of this flower, is so strong he virtually *becomes* the rose in the act of looking at it.

A beginner's mind sees what is in front of it and is very appreciative, very grateful. Prescience (ironically) as well as concentration are called for. Thoreau insisted that the "Scarlet oak must, in a sense, be in your eye when you go forth."

What we see is likewise related to what we don't

see. *The New York Times* obituary of Joyce Wethered, described by *The Encyclopedia of Golf* as "the supreme woman golfer of her age, perhaps of all time," provided this enlightening anecdote of her. Once Ms. Wethered was about to hit a nine-foot putt on the seventeenth hole at the Sheringham course in Norfolk, when a train rumbled by within 100 yards. She sank the putt. When her playing partner expressed surprise, she seemed baffled. "What train?" she remarked.

Via intuitive seeing, a writer sees the unseeable. Real becomes non-real; non-real real. Her third eye pierces the invisible, even as her temporal eyes simply stay focused on whatever is before them.

"ASHES DO NOT
COME BACK TO
FIREWOOD"

*I think that any true work of art does defuse
criticism; if it left anything important to be
said, it wouldn't be doing its job.*
                                    —JOHN ASHBERY

*My life is, in a sense, trash; my life is only
that of which the residue is my writing.*
                                    —JOHN UPDIKE

"Zen activity is activity that is completely burned out.
Nothing remains but ashes. This is what Dogen
meant," Suzuki-roshi told us, when he said, " 'Ashes
do not come back to firewood.' If you do not burn
yourself completely, a trace of yourself will be left in
what you do."

Burn yourself completely? Isn't that a formula for stress? Ironically it's just the opposite. Stress comes with resistance, when there is a "no" lurking in our behavior. The "no" acts like a barrier keeping a part of us at a distance. When we "burn ourselves completely" we sear the part that prevents us from being wholehearted.

In a Zen kitchen, leftovers from breakfast and lunch are added to a grain that along with vegetables in a second bowl, comprise dinner. Leftovers from that are kneaded into bread. Every scrap is accounted for.

Or seen. One reason to be mindful is to see. Mindfulness changes you as well as your surroundings and the people (for writers this includes potential readers) who have access to those surroundings.

The Zen-monastic meal ritual is tight as a drum. Nothing is taken for granted. Nothing is extra. Nothing is wasted. Our writing practice should be like that.

Tightening your writing and tightening your writing practice requires ongoing endless effort. In your revision periods, for example, as soon as you "see" that something doesn't work or isn't needed, get rid of it. As Suzuki-roshi used to say about getting up when the alarm rings, "Never make the same decision twice."

LADY MURASAKI'S

INSIGHT

❦

*The distinction between a thing well done and
a thing done ill obtains everywhere—in all
circles of Paradise and Inferno.*
                                        —JOHN UPDIKE

In *The Tale of Genji*, Lady Murasaki suddenly becomes aware of a new object of interest in her lover's,
Prince Genji's, life. One morning while they are still
in bed, a messenger delivers to Genji a letter from
the young woman. All of Lady Murasaki's fears, heretofore considerable, instantly fall away when she
glimpses the girl's handwriting. She knows Genji well
enough to be sure that no matter how sensual he
finds the youth, her shallow inner life, transparent in
her penmanship, will not please him.

"Transparent in her penmanship"—that's the key
phrase. We try to convince ourselves that a lowering

of consciousness won't show. "No one will notice," we assure ourselves, knowing full well that even candy-bar makers don't get away with it.

In the early years of their relationship Georgia O'Keeffe gave Alfred Stieglitz an urn. Finding it unhandsome, Stieglitz smashed it to pieces. "These things spread," he said, referring to the urn's less-than-perfect craftsmanship. The vibrations of an item immaculately conceived are very different from those conceived hastily or from a sluggish mind. If we are surrounded by mediocrity, even while we sleep, it will make inroads on our aesthetic sensibility.

"The hawk sat on a limb three feet above my head and did not stir as I walked under—that was the first sign." Bill McKibben's evocative one-liner opens the introduction to his annotated edition of *Walden*.

McKibben had been hiking for about a week in the Adirondacks. No radio, t.v., newspaper. ". . . The stocks of mental junk food were starting to dwindle; . . . the buzz turned to hum, and once in a while to quiet . . . and so I was not completely surprised when the hawk kept his perch, or a few minutes later when I passed a pair of grazing deer and they merely looked up a moment, didn't spook."

That night I was aware of every second of the endless sunset: the first long rays of the sun as the afternoon turned late, the long twilight, the turn of the sky from blue to blue to blue to—just as it turned black, a heron came stalking through my tiny cove, standing silently and then spearing with a sudden spasm; I couldn't see her, not really, but I knew where she was. The sky darkened, the stars in this dark place spread across the sky bright and insistent. We were unimaginably small, this heron and I, and extremely *right*.[42]

Small *is* "right" and McKibben's difficult-to-achieve inner stillness is "right." (The hawk and the deer both got it.)

But how do we elucidate silence/stillness with words?

"A cottage over the valley, a window facing the
    hills, soundless and barren.
Who could know there are human affairs in the
    valley?
From the town when you look out
you see only empty clouds and the mountains."

—WANG WEI

In their critical introduction to the *Poems of Wang Wei*, Willis and Tony Barnstone, who refer to Wang Wei as the quietest poet in Chinese and perhaps in all literary history, say that the voices one hears in his poetry are those one hears in absolute silence. For Wang Wei, silence becomes both a discipline and the subject matter of his poems. Indeed, the Barn-stones point out, in Wang Wei's poems there are three kinds of silence. The first is physical, the silence of the outer world. This quiet world is a precondition for the second silence which is spiritual, the silence of the mind. Which mind, purged of distractions, prepares one for the third silence, the silence of mystical meditation. "When thought stops, words halt, and we move through light toward absolute stillness."[43]

"Without silence, solitude, darkness, how can we come to any sense of our true size, our actual relationship with the rest of the world?," McKibben asks. Or, we might add, with the "zone of silence in the middle of every art"? ". . . when someone is whispering something in your ear, there's no way to think your own thoughts or feel your own responses."

Stillness shrinks us to our own size, empowers us to acknowledge our pain, lends us the air into which this pain can, momentarily, evaporate.

When silence is used to fill words and the gaps between words, the ordinary understanding of what is needed to convey meaning entirely changes.

Although Suzuki [Shunryu Suzuki-roshi] told Cage [John Cage] that he had nothing to say about music or art, Cage still felt Suzuki had led him to see music "not as a communication from the artist to an audience, but rather as an activity of sounds in which the artist found a way to let the sounds be themselves."

Silence fosters immediacy in language. In its ultimate form, silence is what language is intended to elucidate.

In my poem "The Intimacy of the Silence" the subject is saturated language—how a writer infuses words with her own kind of silence and how this in turn creates her "voice."

The Intimacy of the Silence

To saturate is to satisfy fully
to load to capacity
to fill completely
with something that permeates
an indistinct plentitude which is empty.

To saturate language
a writer must
silence herself
so that the word
pure passivity of being
is.
She stiffened a little
on the kerb,
waiting for Durtnall's van
to pass.[44]

Blanchot explains that
tone is not the writer's voice,
but the *intimacy of the silence*
she imposes upon the word.
He was gazing earnestly
at the little boy.[45]

The silence is still his.
He preserves himself
within the work.

At night
she would doze off
with morphine
and my mother and Grandpa
each drank
in their separate rooms.[46]

Silence is felt as concentration.
There she was perched,
never seeing him,
waiting to cross
very upright.[47]
Movement within something enclosed.
A small action
or detail
with elaborate internal activity.

Logic is tension
and tension is transparent.
He threw coffee on the fires,
staining the plastic-soft floor
a deep cave brown.[48]

Breakups in a contextual,
denotative or linguistic sense
do not affect
the stream of concentration
continuity
which pushes the skin of a word
so that
saturated
it will stand alone
Don't you notice
something rather different
about his eyes?[49]
like a full balloon
can support itself.

THE FRIDA KAHLO

PRINCIPLE

. . . Like stokers knowing only their own fur-
naces, whatever might be happening on deck
or at sea, writers should occupy themselves
only with their own meaningless, innocent, in-
toxicating business. . . .

—VLADIMIR NABOKOV[50]

Many of Frida Kahlo's self-portraits were painted while she lay in a supine post-surgery position staring into a mirror affixed to her bed-post. First she painted her external self, then her feelings, then met-aphorical and symbolical portrayals of her feelings. The more deeply she penetrated her interior life, the more grounded she became in the human condition, the place where we connect with our own as well as all forms of suffering. The more graphically she de-scribed the details of her own particulars, the more universal these particulars grew. Nearly everyone can locate herself in Frida Kahlo's pain.

The greater the depth at which you tap your own personal truth, the greater relevance your writing will have to humanity.

AN ANGEL IN
THE HOUSE

Virginia Woolf had to throw an ink pot at her Victorian mother/editor (her "Angel in the House") who slipped behind her "in rustling skirts" reminding her to be "charming, tender and polite" before she could find her writer's voice. Whereas angels are perfect, humans are in constant need of correction. It gets tiresome.

Writers enter the Angel-versus-me fray with a handicap. An Angel "knows" she's right. Thus she stands for "truth" while the writer probably thinks there is something the matter with her. More likely, the writer is just feeling her particularly well-developed feelings.

Feelings themselves are neither good nor bad. It is what we learn from them that make them so valuable. Especially for a writer who not only needs to know herself before she can tackle any other subject, but whose subject will be grounded in what she knows and can articulate about her feelings.

Human beings are holistic. Each part, filtering down through layer after layer of perception and reflection, enriches and nourishes all the other parts. Your best weapon against an "Angel in the House" is self-immersion. You silence her by sinking into your own fathomless silence.

FEELINGS AND CHARACTER TRAITS APPROPRIATE AND USEFUL FOR A WRITER

Even if it just leads you to affirm, "That's not how it is for me, *this* is how it is"—well, upholding who you are is the point of reviewing the following list of feelings and character traits that writers sometimes are wont to find intimidating:

- excitement (the low-grade churning kind): When hounds are on a fox's trail, they are very energetic, very roused, even if the fox is nowhere in the vicinity.
- intoxication (a "high"): While the rush that you

feel is important for its power to propel you forward, it isn't always necessary to keep the vehicle that got you there. Painful though it seems, sometimes what you write is primarily significant for what it leads you to write *next*.

- boredom: Not always, but in many cases, a writer's boredom says, "Dead language reflects dead thought." Just as a Geiger counter registers lethal radiation, a writer learns to recognize those elements that contaminate the pure energy of her writing.
  - illegitimacy: If you feel illegitimate around your writing, it can mean that you are right on track— innovative, wild, extreme—yes.
- "too" sensitive: Sensitivity for a writer is the same as speed for a runner or legerdemain for a juggler. The only way a writer can be "too" sensitive is if her sensitivity prevents her from writing.
- self-conscious: Self-consciousness, which stems from a deprivation—from not being seen, acknowledged and validated at critical developmental moments, sabotages authenticity. Self-honesty is the antidote. Along with regular daily writing periods.
- solipsistic ("intense," "preoccupied," "self-absorbed"): A writer is only as strong as the connection she maintains with herself.

- anxious (perfectionistic/fussy): This is part of a writer's understandable instinct for self-preservation.

- conflictual: Writers fight a myriad of internal battles that are difficult to translate to other people. For example, they often have low self-esteem coupled with an odd form of grandiosity (John Barth: "It's a combination of an almost obscene self-confidence and an ongoing terror."); they are intelligent but in unmeasurable ways (they don't test well and frequently have unconventional educations); they are highly skilled yet have difficulty finding congenial work in the world; they are easy-going in their lifestyle yet have unusual and non-negotiable needs; they have off-beat yet distinctive tastes; they enjoy people but are fierce about time alone; they are likable but peculiar. (Excuse the generalizations.)

- pained: We all experience both joy and pain but, as Anne Sexton says, "pain engraves a deeper memory."

- rigid: "Too controlling" or "too picky" are not uncommon criticisms for a writer to hear about herself, yet what is the difference between that and wanting *your* vision realized?

NOT KNOWING

There is no need to have a deep understanding of Zen, Suzuki-roshi used to say. When you read Zen literature, you must read each sentence with a fresh mind. Writing is the same. The real work of writing is, day after day, to discover *how* to maintain freshness.

"Not knowing" is a way. It is very respectful. "Not knowing" assumes that the object of your curiosity is always new and worthy of your entire attention.

For a writer, "not knowing" means giving over the part of you that knows to the writing. The writing tells *you* what it is (you have to listen carefully). When a piece tells you it's finished you say, "Oh!" (By this time all your "great ideas" will probably have been obliterated.)

> . . . the only meanings that are worth anything in a work of art are those that the artist himself knows nothing about. The moment the artist tries to ex-

press *his* ideas and *his* emotions he misses the great thing.[51]

Jorge Luis Borges agreed. Poetry springs from something deeper than intelligence. You can't nail writing down and use it as you want. You have to let *it* use *you*.

When John Barth was planning *Sabbatical*, he knew that something climactic had to happen in the next to last chapter but he had no idea what it would be until he found himself—whoops—at the next to last chapter.

T.S. Eliot, likewise, said, "I never think more than one step ahead." A writer follows his writing like a blindfolded person thrashes the air before taking the next baby-step forward.

". . . Theory organizes experience prematurely, thus giving it the theory's shape."[52] A "great idea" (by taking charge, preempting the spontaneous) can interfere with you connecting with a subtler and potentially more amazing part of yourself.

To avoid short-circuiting this connection, I recommend "unfocused listening," a kind of musing whereby you become immersed in your interior life. To bypass preconceived ideas, consciously cultivate stillness, then notice what crystallizes out of your reverie.

> But this is only my old grumble, that we are afraid of the human heart (and with reason); and until we can write with all our faculties in action (even the big toe) but under the water, submerged, then we must be clever, like the rest of the modern sticklebacks.[53]

What is the best way to write? Each of us has to discover her own way by writing. Writing teaches writing. No one can tell you your own secret.

ONE WORLD AT

A TIME

Mihaly Cskiszentmihalyi, a psychologist at the University of Chicago, has developed a theory of optimal inner experience based on the concept of "flow," which he defines as a state of utter engrossment. In this state, a person becomes so deeply absorbed in an activity that nothing else matters. Contrary to what we usually believe, our best moments occur when our body or mind is stretched to its limits in a voluntary effort to accomplish something difficult and worthwhile, Cskiszentmihalyi contends. Happiness, therefore, is something we can *make* happen by becoming one with whatever we are doing.

Suzuki-roshi says, ". . . if you limit your activity to what you can do just now, in this moment, then you can express fully your true nature, which is the universal Buddha nature."[54]

"Limiting your activity to what you can do just now" includes both contracting and intensifying.

Painter Walter Sickert was admired for living "at such a pitch of awareness [it was] as if he remembered death at all times." Monks routinely meditate in cemeteries to instill the same lesson. Why would that make you happy? Because both body and mind are fully engaged, stretched to their limits of understanding.

> [Thomas] Hardy's work—and her [Virginia Woolf's] meeting with him—confirmed her sense that in fiction, as in autobiography and biography, it was the "moments of great intensity," which counted and told all.[55]

Thoreau based his life on this principle. A few days before he died, a visitor asked, "You seem so near the brink of the dark river that I almost wonder how the opposite shore may appear to you." His answer: "One world at a time."

APPENDICES

GUIDELINES FOR BEGINNING WRITERS OF HAIKU

A successful haiku works on three levels:

1. the surface, literal level pleases and is enticing;
2. underneath, a deeper layer of meaning emerges;
3. finally, if a reader is receptive, the haiku will create the space for a moment of enlighten-ment:

> fallout —
> a radio blares
> through the empty hallway

LEVEL ONE: THE POEM'S SURFACE

1. Many of us have been taught that haiku, by definition, are short poems of seventeen syllables written in three lines of five-seven-five syllables respectively. This may be so for most haiku written in

Japanese, but Japanese syllables are weightier and function differently from English syllables. Generally, it is more important to focus on capturing the *essence* of a "haiku moment" (the instantaneous *now*) than on squeezing your poem into a preset number of syllables. However, it is also acceptable to use seventeen syllables if that format helps you.

winter sun —
pale wings
flutter about the woodpile

2. Try to use precise, compelling sense impressions (taste, touch, sight, sound, smell):

snow buries
the leaf tips —
watch

3. Try to stay in the first person. Should you choose to employ a noun or a second or third person pronoun, understand the effect you are able to create that you would not be able to create by other means.

> noisy city
> the old woman
> lost in her peach

Were you to use first person ("and me/lost in my peach") you would sacrifice the poignant implication of an old woman having little refuge for her growing need for solace.

4. Aim for the present (not past or future) and the instant (not hour or day). In other words, stay with what can be known (not guessed or surmised).

> night falls
> I watch
> door ajar

5. Each line should have integrity with smooth-flowing, carefully positioned pauses (one pause tends to be more effective than two) and should, poetically-speaking, stand on its own.
6. Use punctuation conscientiously and sparingly. Also consider alternatives to punctuation such as indentations. These are very striking because they add a visual component.

                    big blue butterfly

                        past my eyes and

                    out

                            to

                                sea

7. Avoid rhetorical devices (such as simile, metaphor, anthropomorphisms), concepts, abstractions,
stated interpretations, speculations, ideas, and beliefs.
These substitute the characteristics of one entity for
another at the expense of naturalness and authenticity.

LEVEL TWO: A DEEPER LAYER OF MEANING

1. *Show* readers what you experience so they can
have the same experience on their own, bringing
to it their own history and inner life—don't tell
them.

2. Try taking *out* the main subject (so that it is
implied instead).

                    sudden squall —

                    my hands

                    wrap around the teacup

The main subject of this haiku is a state of mind—anxiety, nervousness, a sense of foreboding, which is not stated. A description of a behavior is used instead to *imply* the state of mind. This leaves a gap for readers to fill in.

3. Try approaching your subject from right angles instead of head on so as to see it more freshly.

> autumn leaves
> lie quietly
> in the sun

"This is nothing" a reader could think, not noticing that beneath the disarmingly modest exterior is a poem about stillness, about the nature of impermanence, about surrender, about the Buddha's teaching of dependent co-arising.[56]

4. Ambiguity is good if it is suggestive but not if it belies or misleads the reader.

> a train whistle blows —
> perched in a tree
> crow closes its eyes

We know from this poem that there is a train, a crow and a tree. Otherwise it could be anywhere, any hour, any season, any year. The ambiguity allows a reader to bring her own mnemonica to bear on the strong feeling of loneliness evoked by the setting.

Sometimes ambiguity is less general, targeting either one or both of only two interpretations. In these cases the poet must be sure that both possible ways of seeing the situation enhance rather than detract from the overall strength of the poem's subject.

> bending over
> the frog's grave —
> cherry blossoms

The fact that the poem leaves open for interpretation whether it is a person or a cherry tree or both bending over the grave strengthens the pathos of the setting. However, consider the following:

> draped over a stone —
> are you dead yet
> little goldfish

The question arises, is the persona maliciously killing the fish or merely reporting on a death he or she finds agonizing to watch? If the subject of the poem is compassion, the possibility of the former interpretation notably weakens its cause. It would have been better if the poet phrased the description in such a way that an unkind motivation was inconceivable.

5. Provide a context for your sense impressions whenever possible.

> silent snow
> silent house
> I stand in the moonlit doorway

The poem is about silence—silence in the objective world, silence in the subjective world and the ultimate silence of transcendence. The doorway functions as a transitional space between these three universes, which is what is meant by "context." The immensity of the subject is grounded by one small, very particular detail.

LEVEL THREE: A POTENTIAL MOMENT OF ENLIGHTENMENT

1. Regarding the need for a poet to become fully immersed in the experience of a poem, haiku master Bashō had this to say:

> A lucid description of the object is not enough; unless the poem contains feelings which have spontaneously emerged from the object, it will show the object and the poet's self as two separate entities, making it impossible to attain a true poetic sentiment. The poem will be artificial, for it is composed by the poet's personal self.[57]

Full immersion is the element of haiku-writing that can become, in Bashō's words, "a vehicle for entering the True Way."

2. Stay in your moment until it suffuses you. Don't rush to write. Freezing your inspiration into an idea *before* you begin to write, can short-circuit the essence of your "moment."

3. Many of the above guidelines have to do with creating space for a reader to bring his experience to bear upon the poem. Careful juxtaposition of ele-

ments in a poem—positioning them so that a reader is forced to make a leap, i.e. to reconcile some tension be it from disparate images, tones, sounds, or from an unexpected descriptive word or pairing of different aspects of an experience—is one way of creating space. While a full discussion of juxtaposition is beyond the scope of these guidelines, writers should not lose sight of (and ideally learn to recognize and build) poetic power from careful placement of their haiku's constituent parts.

> the wind blows stronger —
> old women rustle through
> piles of free clothes

Exercise: Since the true depth of haiku reveals itself most fully within the context of a daily writing practice, you might experiment with dedicating a specified period of time (say six months) to writing one haiku a day. Keep them together in a small notebook. Each day, after drafting your new haiku, review your previous poems. Revisiting experiences recorded earlier allows you continually to refine the rendering of your "haiku moment." If you find a partner who is also practicing a daily poem, you can exchange work—increase your objectivity and clarity.

A man of awe-inspiring diligence, he [Pliny] had books read to him while he ate, while he traveled, and indeed at all times except when he bathed. Even then, the reading was stopped only for the actual immersion. The reading resumed while he was being toweled and rubbed. Pliny took notes and made extracts on all he read, saying no book was so bad as to have nothing of value.[58]

What is your relationship with reading? Just as there are distinct personality and body types, there are distinct reading types—groups of people who can be identified by their reading style. Understanding who you are as a reader will validate your reading choices, make them more meaningful to you.

Some people browse. They enjoy scanning a wide variety of material. They may occasionally read a book in its entirety but for this type of reader, sampling itself is very nourishing.

Some people skim, lightly perusing selected portions of whatever comes their way.

Some people read often and passionately, yet limit their reading to mystery stories or science fiction. Some faithfully and meticulously read magazines, newspapers, and professional journals—but that's all. Some read indiscriminately—ingesting everything (soup can labels, bottle caps) they can lay their hands on. Some consume only what comes highly recommended. Some read for plot, racing to the end to find out "what happened." Some are intoxicated by a particular author's voice and can never get enough of it. Some are gripped by whatever they can find on their (often) esoteric area of expertise. For a few, life and library are one. The great English Benedictine monk, Bede Griffiths, describes in his autobiography, *The Golden String*, how he made a path out of practicing what he read.

Some people read like other people drink. A romance novel can be sipped like a glass of fine wine, carefully chosen and anticipated. Coleridge and Thoreau were both chain readers. One book led to another which led to still others. Mary Emerson (Ralph Waldo's irascible aunt) says she read "zigzag" through fields, authors, and even single books. John Henry Newman went to "reading parties." (Groups of Oxford men retired to the country and simply read for the weekend!)

Academics are reading gymnasts. Some can maneuver their way to the essence of the most complicated book in less than five minutes. Some consider it a waste of time to read any book in its entirety. Some read for the interpretation and once that is grasped, find the rest of little value. Some have developed an elaborate system of note-taking and can quickly reference every item they have ever read.

In the Christian monastic tradition, *lectio divina* (sacred reading) is a means of engaging oneself in a transformative relationship with scripture. Immersing oneself in a text, reading slowly, opening one's heart along with one's mind, becomes a form of prayer, a time-honored path toward wisdom and compassion.[59]

A READING-PREFERENCE ASSESSMENT TEST

Can you find yourself in the above descriptions of reading styles? What about your reading preferences? For one month, track your choices: genial reading (pleasant, light); academic reading; mindless reading (less straining even than genial reading); informational reading; "deep" reading (religion, philosophy, poetry); inspirational reading (biography or autobiography); author-focused reading; spiritual reading; vacation reading; wacky reading; fun reading; shopping reading; newspaper/newsmagazine reading; nostalgic reading; voyeuristic reading; self-help reading; how-to reading; life-sustaining reading; "I-wish" reading; travel reading and/or consciousness-raising reading.

*Each new mind we approach seems to require
an abdication of all our past and present em-
pire. A new doctrine seems at first a subver-
sion of all our opinions, tastes, and manner
of living.*

— BRONSON ALCOTT

*All men together progress continually while
the universe grows older . . . so that the whole
succession of men throughout the centuries
should be considered as one and the same man
who lives for ever and continually learns.*

— PASCAL from *Traité du Vide*

By introducing the unfamiliar, learning can occasionally feel uncomfortable. We want to change and grow,
yet at the same time, we resist change and growth.
There is bound to be a struggle (or, in Chögyam
Trungpa Rinpoche's words, a "natural repulsion")

no matter how enthusiastic the learner is at the outset.

Because writers need constantly to be learning—about themselves, their craft, their subject—and because having things "pointed out," being "corrected" and so forth is painful (de-integration is a necessary part of change), it is incumbent on a writer to consciously keep her learning channels open. Identifying worn-out learning stances, therefore, is an important form of personal housecleaning.

We all carry vestiges of habits that once served us well. Can you find yourself anywhere in the following digest of learning habits?

1. *Painfully Self-Conscious:* You have been traumatized by previous harsh judgment. As if you fear you will contaminate whatever you touch, it is hard for you to imagine any response other than a negative one to a product of your efforts.

2. *Painfully Invisible:* You have been traumatized by years of not being seen. For example, you may be the one art-oriented person in a family of scientists or the only literary person in a group of business-minded peers. As odd-woman-out you have designed a sophis-

ticated series of pain-management tactics. You may try very little—do the bare minimum—not even bother perusing a teacher's feedback.

3. *Scattered:* For the scattered learner, anything becomes a distraction, sometimes for days, possibly years.

4. *One-Up:* You become overtly or covertly competitive, derogatory or inflated in an effort to deny (or deflect) the impact of criticism.

5. *Macho:* You learn primarily by demonstrating what you know. Only after making an effort first yourself, will you welcome a suggestion from someone else.

6. *An A is an A is an A:* You are frankly out for an "A." You aren't interested in learning. You're interested in excelling, though learning may be a secondary benefit.

7. *I Hardly Cracked a Book:* You truly *want* to learn but feel embarrassed about it, so surrounded are you by gamesmanship. You might stay up all night studying then tell your friends you're unprepared. "Gosh. I hardly cracked a book!"

8. *Maverick:* You are independent-minded and need to do things your own way. Listening to

others (even their good advice) smacks of a "party line."

9. *Love-Starved:* You do magnificently as the teacher's pet but if your position is usurped, you lose your confidence.

10. *Vulnerable:* You identify and relay all your weaknesses first so no one else can accuse you of making a mistake.

11. *Diligent But . . . :* You try very hard and can see that you are making progress, but a sense of mastery endlessly eludes you.

12. *Shy:* You take a secondary as opposed to a primary role in your learning process. Your teacher formulates, you acquiesce.

13. *Abused:* You carry a pervasive sense of being incompetent. Though you ask a lot of questions, the answers don't make sense. It is as if you need soothing more than information. In some cases you may not actually be stable enough to learn, i.e., receive constructive feedback and use it for your growth.

If you recognize a part of yourself in one or more of the above patterns (or you may simply recognize a strong resistance to recognizing yourself), watch and record what you notice, allowing yourself, in a compassionate, non-judgmental way, to feel the feelings that arise. The more you bring them to consciousness, the more they will lose their power and the more you will find yourself increasingly capable of making healthier choices around learning behaviors.

NOTES

1. David Schneider, *Street Zen*, 168.
2. Hermione Lee, *Virginia Woolf*, 170.
3. "Grandmother's finger pointing," a particular term of the Kagyü tradition of Tibetan Buddhism, means showing one how to do it.
4. *A Healing Family*, 58.
5. Robert D. Richardson Jr., *Emerson: The Mind on Fire*, 42.
6. Richardson, *Thoreau*, 107.
7. Brian Boyd, *The American Years*, 31.
8. Hermione Lee, *Virginia Woolf*, 212.
9. Ibid., 408.
10. Robert D. Richardson Jr., *Emerson: The Mind on Fire*, 163.
11. Makoto, Ueda, *Modern Japanese Poets and the Nature of Literature*, 235.
12. Brian Boyd, *The Russian Years*, 276.
13. Ibid., 418.
14. Edward Espe Brown, *Tomato Blessings and Radish Teachings*, 196.
15. David Schneider, *Street Zen*, 104.

16. I am indebted to Bonnie Friedman for the concept "writer's anorexia."

17. Ronald Fairbairn, a great Scots psychoanalyst, originated the phrase "internal saboteur."

18. Robert Aitken, *Original Dwelling Place*, 134.

19. Dom Bede Griffiths, *Marriage of East and West*, 62–63.

20. A Nabokovian thought presented by Brian Boyd, *The Russian Years*, 12.

21. Boyd, *The American Years*, 585–86.

22. Adam Phillips, *Winnicott*, 16.

23. Richardson, *Thoreau*, 215.

24. Ibid., 95.

25. Lee, *Virginia Woolf*, 19.

26. Ibid., 404.

27. Quoted by Brian Boyd, *The Russian Years*, 51–52.

28. Ibid., 58.

29. Ibid., 470.

30. Lee, *Virginia Woolf*, 427.

31. (1) James Joyce, *Dubliners*

    (2) William Trevor, *Reading Turgenev*

    (3) Dylan Thomas, *Portrait of an Artist as a Young Dog*

    (4) Virginia Woolf, *To the Lighthouse*

    (5) Samuel Beckett, *Graphophone Nickelodeon Days*

    (6) Nathaniel Hawthorne, *The Scarlet Letter*

    (7) John Steinbeck, *The Grapes of Wrath*

    (8) Willa Cather, *My Ántonia*

32. Vladimir Nabokov quoted by Brian Boyd, *The American Years*, 112.

33. Brenda Wineapple, *Sister Brother: Gertrude and Leo Stein*, 360.

34. ———. 354.

35. Henry David Thoreau, *Faith in a Seed*, xvi.

36. I am indebted to Gareth Hill who pointed out Wayne K. Detloff's article, "A Study of Authors with Reflections on Language and Jung's Typology" in *The Shaman From Elko* published by The San Francisco Jung Institute and edited by Gareth Hill, 1978.

37. Dom Bede Griffiths, *Marriage of East and West*, 63.

38. Heinz Kohut founded Self Psychology, a new school within psychoanalysis that emphasizes the effect of relationships on our developing sense of self.

39. Heinz Kohut, *The Restoration of the Self*, 285, 286, 288.

40. A phrase on a Sierra Club Legal Defense Fund bumper sticker to describe endangered species.

41. Walter Harding, *The Days of Henry Thoreau*, 27.

42. Bill McKibben (ed.), *Walden*, viii.

43. Tony and Willis Barnstone, *The Poems of Wang Wei*, xliv.

44. Woolf, *Mrs. Dalloway*, 1925.

45. Lady Murasaki, *The Tale of Genji*, 1976.

46. Lucia Berlin, "Dr. H. A. Moynihan" from *Phantom Pain*.

47. Woolf, *Mrs. Dalloway*, 1925.

48. Berlin, "Dr. H. A. Moynihan" from *Phantom Pain*.

49. Lady Murasaki, *The Tale of Genji*, 1976.

50. Boyd, *The Russian Years*, 409.

51. Lee, *Virginia Woolf*, 465.

52. Kim Chernin, *A Different Kind of Listening*, 64.

53. Lee, *Virginia Woolf*, 642.

54. Shunryu Suzuki, *Zen Mind, Beginner's Mind*, 75.

55. Lee, *Virginia Woolf*, 532.

56. That everything comes forth from all directions in the universe to make each thing, and that this coming forth is what gives each thing authority.

57. Makoto Ueda, *Matsuo Bashō* (Twayne Publishers, 1970).

58. Richardson Jr., *Henry Thoreau: A Life of the Mind*, 374–75.

59. Michael Casey, *Sacred Reading, The Ancient Art of Lectio Divina*, 3–4.

BIBLIOGRAPHY

Aitken, Robert. *Original Dwelling Place.* Counterpoint: Washington, D.C., 1996.

Anderson, Tenshin Reb. *Warm Smiles from Cold Mountains.* San Francisco Zen Center: San Francisco, 1995.

Barnstone, Willis and Tony. *Poems of Wang Wei.* University Press of New England: Hanover, N.H., 1991.

Boyd, Brian. *Vladimir Nabokov: The Russian Years.* Princeton University Press: Princeton, N.J., 1990.

———. *Vladimir Nabokov: The American Years.* Princeton University Press: Princeton, N.J., 1991.

Brown, Edward Espe. *Tomato Blessings and Radish Teachings.* Riverhead Books: New York, 1997.

Casey, Michael. *Sacred Reading: The Ancient Art of* Lectio Divina. Triumph Books: Liguori, Mo., 1996.

Chernin, Kim. *A Different Kind of Listening.* HarperCollins: New York, 1995.

Chiari, Joseph. *T.S. Eliot: A Memoir.* The Enitharmon Press: London, 1982.

Cskiszentmihalyi, Mihaly. *Flow.* HarperCollins: New York, 1990.

Friedman, Bonnie. *Writing Past Dark: Envy, Fear, Distrac-*

tion, and Other Dilemmas in the Writer's Life. Harper-Collins: New York, 1993.

Griffiths, Dom Bede. *Marriage of East and West.* Temple-gate: Springfield, Ill., 1982.

Harding, Walter. *The Days of Henry Thoreau: A Biography.* Princeton University Press: Princeton, N.J., 1992.

Kapleau, Philip. *Awakening to Zen.* Scribner: New York, 1997.

Lee, Hermione. *Virginia Woolf.* Knopf: New York, 1997.

McKibben, Bill (ed.). *Walden.* Beacon Press: Boston, 1997.

Oë, Kenzaburo. *A Healing Family.* Kodansha International: New York, 1996.

Phillips, Adam. *Winnicott.* Harvard University Press: Cambridge, Mass., 1988.

Richardson, Robert D. Jr. *Emerson: The Mind on Fire.* University of California Press: Berkeley, 1995.

———. *Henry Thoreau: A Life of the Mind.* University of California Press: Berkeley, 1986.

Ryan, Joan. *Little Girls in Pretty Boxes.* Doubleday: New York, 1995.

Schneider, David. *Street Zen: The Life and Work of Issan Dorsey.* Shambhala: Boston, 1993.

Suzuki, Shunryu. *Zen Mind, Beginner's Mind.* Weatherhill: New York, 1970.

Thoreau, Henry David. *Faith in a Seed.* Island Press: Washington, D.C., 1993.

Ueda, Makoto. *Modern Japanese Poets and the Nature of Literature.* Stanford University Press: Stanford, Calif., 1983.

Wineapple, Brenda. *Sister Brother: Gertrude and Leo Stein.* G.P. Putnam's Sons: New York, 1996.

4

HO-KYUNG YEO

Honey Mustard Vol. 4
created by Ho-Kyung Yeo

Translation - Jihae Hong
English Adaptation - Jamie S. Rich
Copy Editors - Hope Donovan and Peter Ahlstrom
Retouch and Lettering - Jennifer Carbajal
Production Artist - Jennifer Carbajal
Cover Design - Thea Willis

Editor - Carol Fox
Digital Imaging Manager - Chris Buford
Managing Editor - Lindsey Johnston
Editor-in-Chief - Rob Tokar
VP of Production - Ron Klamert
Publisher - Mike Kiley
President and C.O.O. - John Parker
C.E.O. and Chief Creative Officer - Stu Levy

A  Manga

TOKYOPOP Inc.
5900 Wilshire Blvd. Suite 2000
Los Angeles, CA 90036

E-mail: info@TOKYOPOP.com
Come visit us online at www.TOKYOPOP.com

ISBN: 1-59816-208-X

First TOKYOPOP printing: June 2006
10 9 8 7 6 5 4 3 2 1
Printed in the USA

4

HAMBURG // LONDON // LOS ANGELES // TOKYO

Ara had a crush on the school hottie, Jung Hanil--but through a misunderstanding involving mistaken identity and way too much alcohol, she ended up confessing her love to hapless misfit Young-Woo instead. And just as she planted a kiss on him, the two were caught by the school's puritanical chaperone.

Ara's family was ashamed of her, and Young-Woo's would only be appeased if the two got married. Neither of them wanted to, but when Young-Woo intercepted what he thought was a suicide note from Ara, he desperately proposed marriage to her as an alternative to death. Preferring it to life with her own family, Ara agreed. And before you could say "marriage license," the deal was sealed.

With that, the not-so-happy couple moved to a new school and a tiny apartment. But though they had a marriage license, Young-Woo treated Ara like a stranger. Still, over time, Young-Woo began to grow on Ara--especially when the two of them had to weather an extended visit from Young-Woo's ultra-tough mother. So when Jung Hanil approached her, hoping to make up for his role in Ara's untimely marriage, she realized Young-Woo was the one she truly had feelings for.

But through it all, Ara's jealous stepsister Somi (who, as luck would have it, attends Ara and Young-Woo's new school) has been watching Ara carefully. If Ara shows one sign of happiness, you can bet that Somi will be there to burst it!

Honey MUSTARD™   Album 4

Virus...19

Of the Same Mind...37

The Two of Us...65

The Truth is
Discovered...91

A Crisis...129

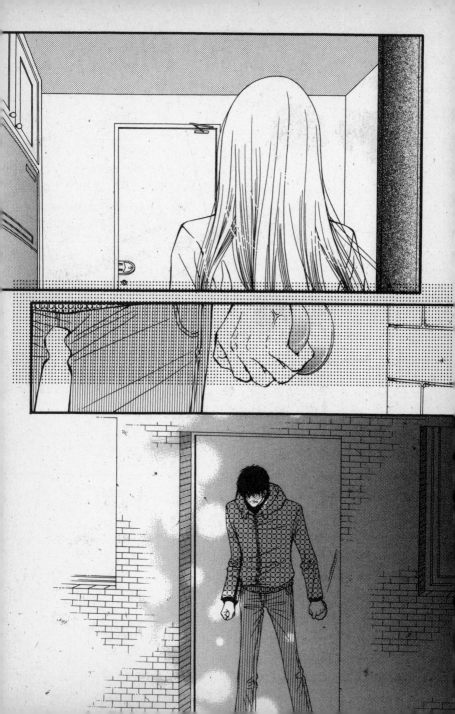

"DON'T TOUCH ME!"

WHY?!

AT FIRST I THOUGHT I HAD SOMETHING ICKY ON MY HAND...

AFTER ALL THIS TIME, HE STILL DOESN'T LIKE ME?

"WHATEVER IT IS, I DON'T WANT TO HEAR IT! LEAVE ME ALONE. YOU HEAR ME?!"

BRRRRR... COLD.

THERE'S NO WHERE TO GO... NOT AT THIS HOUR.

AND IT'S ONLY GONNA GET COLDER.

IT WOULD BE EMBAR- RASSING TO GO BACK IN AGAIN. I JUST LEFT....!

엉금 엉금

I REALLY CAN'T FIGURE IT OUT, NO MATTER HOW HARD I THINK ABOUT IT.

SHOULD I JUST ASK HIM DIRECTLY?

YEAH, GET IT OUT IN THE OPEN!

KHANG YOUNG-WOO! MAKE UP YOUR MIND. ARE YOU GOING TO FREEZE TO DEATH OUT HERE OR EAT SOME CROW BACK INSIDE?!

YOU CAN CONFRONT HER! SIMPLY GO INSIDE AND ASK HER, "WHY WERE YOU MEETING WITH HIM?"

EXCEPT...IT'S NOT LIKE I REALLY HAVE ANY RIGHT TO ASK THAT KIND OF QUESTION, BUT SINCE WE *ARE* LIVING TOGETHER...

Picture 19.
Virus

I CAN'T STOP SHIVERING...

IS SHE EVEN WORRIED ABOUT ME? DOES SHE CARE ABOUT ME AT ALL? SO SELFISH--!!

SE'S OFFICE

NO
ANSWER...
HMM...

THE NURSE
DOESN'T SEEM
TO BE HERE.

WHERE
IS YOUNG-WOO,
THEN?

24

28

Cough

THAT GUY'S COUGHING IS NASTY. I'M TRYING TO EAT HERE! CAN'T HE GO TO THE HOSPITAL ALREADY?

HMMM.

THINKING BACK, FROM THAT DAY ON...

AND UP UNTIL NOW...

IT'S BEEN GETTING HARDER.

COULD IT BE...?

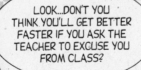

LOOK...DON'T YOU THINK YOU'LL GET BETTER FASTER IF YOU ASK THE TEACHER TO EXCUSE YOU FROM CLASS?

IF YOU GO TO THE DOCTOR, YOU CAN MAYBE GET SOME REST.

EXCUSED FROM CLASS? SO, YOU CAN'T EVEN STAND BEING NEXT TO ME? IS THAT IT?!!

...AND HOW YOUR TEMPERATURE ISN'T GOING DOWN, YOU CAN'T BE TOO CAUTIOUS.

DON'T GET ME WRONG. CONSIDERING HOW BAD I JUST SCREWED UP...

......

I'M JUST WORRIED...

THESE DAYS, COLDS ARE A LOT MORE DANGEROUS, WHAT WITH SARS AND STUFF.

31

Okay, keep repeating the process...

Doctor...

I...I...

......

Picture 20.
Of the Same Mind

NURSE JUNG, TURN ON THE LIGHTS, PLEASE.

NOW, HM...THERE'S NOTHING WRONG INSIDE HIS MOUTH...

THERE ARE NO EVIDENT SIGNS OF WHY HE COLLAPSED, EXCEPT MAYBE HIS EYES HAVE DILATED A LITTLE BIT. AND HE DOES HAVE A TEMPERATURE.

IT'S NOT HIGH ENOUGH TO WORRY ABOUT, THOUGH...

WHAT ARE YOU DOING TO ME--?!

THERE'S NOTHING I CAN'T DO. COME ON, GIVE IT HERE.

THIS... HE...?

DO YOU SEW?

NO, I'M FINE.

IT'LL COME BACK TO HAUNT ME LATER. HE'LL SAY I CAN'T DO MY OWN SEWING IF I GIVE IN NOW. I DON'T CARE HOW HARD IT IS!

HEY, DIDN'T YOU HEAR ME? I SAID I WANT TO HELP.

GIVE IT TO ME! **NOW!!**

NO...I CAN DO IT!

HEY,
THE P.E. TEACHER
SAID EVERYONE SHOULD
HEAD INTO THE GYM. WE'RE
GOING TO BE WORKING ON
PASSING THE BALL
TODAY.

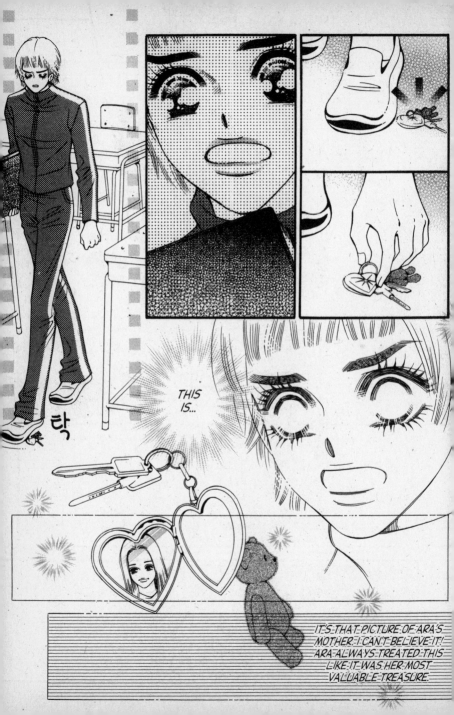

THIS
IS...

IT'S THAT PICTURE OF ARA'S
MOTHER. I CAN'T BELIEVE IT!!
ARA ALWAYS TREATED THIS
LIKE IT WAS HER MOST
VALUABLE TREASURE.

UH, CLASS REPRESENTATIVE! YOU BEAT ME IN HERE. I CAME TO GET THE ATTENDANCE SHEET...

...but you already have it.

I'M SORRY. I KEEP FORGETTING IT...

FORGET ONE MORE TIME AND YOU'RE TOAST!

IT'S OKAY. IT'S EASY TO PICK UP THE SLACK...

LET'S GET BACK TO THE GYM. TEACHER'S WAITING.

UH... OKAY. YEAH, LET'S GO.

스윽

HEE HEE...I CAN'T WAIT TO SEE WHAT THAT BITCH DOES.

So, what are you doing tomorrow?

55

HER STUPID TRINKET--!!

HA! I BET YOU'RE GOING TO GET ALL BENT OUT OF SHAPE OVER IT, GO ARA!

WHAT'S UP WITH THAT? WHY IS SHE TOSSING IT OUT THE WINDOW?

IT'S NOT HERE...

58

59

I JUST FEEL HAPPY TODAY. LIFE IS GOING MY WAY!

!!

IT'S LIKE I HAD THIS WEIGHT ON MY CHEST FOR TEN YEARS, AND IT'S BEEN LIFTED ALL OF A SUDDEN. YOU EVER FEEL ANYTHING LIKE THAT?

NO, SOUNDS AWESOME. WHAT'S GOING ON?

IT...CAN'T BE...

HEY, GO ARA. WAIT HERE FOR ME A SEC--OKAY?

IT'S DARK ALREADY...

SHOULD I JUST GIVE UP AND GO?

Gasp Gasp

!!

DAMN, IT WAS HARDER TO FIND THAN I THOUGHT, BUT IS THIS IT?

64

Picture 21.
The Two of Us

THEN START TALKING! WHY DID YOU THROW AWAY GO ARA'S KEYCHAIN?

WH-WHAT DOES THAT HAVE TO DO WITH ANYTHING?!

AND WHAT *PROOF* DO YOU HAVE THAT I DID THAT?!

FINE. BOOK BAG BECOMES TRASH BAG.

ARGHHH!

IF THAT'S YOUR DECISION...I GUESS THAT'S IT.

튓!

ACKK! NO!! MY BURBERRY BAG!!

YOU'RE SUCH A BULLY! DO YOU KNOW HOW MUCH THAT COSTS? HE TRASHED IT...WHAT DO I DO?! WHAT DO I DO?!

휙

Gasp

I GOTTA DO THIS MORE OFTEN.

I FEEL WEIRD. WHY...?

W-WHAT'S GOING ON? WHY IS KHANG YOUNG-WOO MAKING MOVES ON GO ARA? IT'S CREEPY!!

BRRRR...THIS CLASS BETTER END SOON SO I CAN GET OUT OF THIS FREEZING COLD.

WHY WOULD I WANT TO DO THAT? LEGGO OF ME!

WHY WOULD I WANT TO SEE HER APARTMENT?! I'M ALREADY COMPLETELY HUMILIATED!!

COME ON, JUNG HANIL...

THE LEAST YOU COULD DO IS SHOW US HOW TO GET THERE. WE ONLY HAVE THE ADDRESS, BUT WE DON'T KNOW OUR WAY AROUND. PLEASE, JUNG HANIL...?

I'M ASKING NICELY. PLEASE...?

NO...I CAN'T GIVE IN...I CAN'T DO IT...

TURN HERE, AND THE SECOND HOUSE DOWN HAS A TOP-FLOOR APARTMENT.

...EXCEPT I JUST DID.

THIS IS AS FAR AS I GO. YOU'RE ON YOUR OWN.

He's really going back.

THANKS, JUNG HANIL! WE'LL BE SURE TO SEND YOUR REGARDS TO ARA. BYE!

MiGO

MiGO BakeR

GOTTA GET HOME FAST.

SOON...

feeling
art

HEE HEE...

......!!

83

I CAME HOME DREAMING OF A HAPPY, RELAXING TIME WITH ARA AND ME AND... DAMN...

LOOK...

IT'S PAST MIDNIGHT...ISN'T IT A LITTLE LATE FOR YOU TWO TO BE OUT?

IT'S TOTALLY COOL. I CALLED HOME AND GOT PERMISSION. I CAN STAY OUT UNTIL 2 O'CLOCK.

Grr!

MY MOM SAID I CAN STAY OVER IF I WANT. IT'S BEEN SO LONG, THERE'S A TON WE HAVE TO TALK ABOUT. RIGHT, ARA?

Grrr!

Picture 22.
The Truth is Discovered

93

WHEN DID YOU FIND THE TIME TO WORK FOR EXTRA FUNDS?

THE TRUTH IS FAR TOO TRICKY TO EXPLAIN...

OH, YOU KNOW, HERE AND THERE. IF WE'RE GOING TO BE INDEPENDENT, WE CAN'T GO RUNNING TO MY FAMILY ALL THE TIME.

WELL, ... YOUR GRANDFATHER GAVE ME A SAVINGS ACCOUNT THE OTHER DAY.

I NEVER CONSIDERED HOW TAKING THE MONEY MIGHT AFFECT YOU.

THE SAVINGS BOOK IS IN THE DRESSER DRAWER. TAKE IT. I'LL...I'LL GO AHEAD AND GO TO SCHOOL FIRST TODAY AND LEAVE YOU TO IT.

100

106

107

I SHOULDN'T HAVE GOTTEN SO ANGRY.

I SHOULDN'T HAVE BEEN SO ACCUSATORY.

WHERE CAN YOU BE?

IN THIS RAIN, WHERE WOULD YOU GO TO GET DRY?

THE RAIN ISN'T STOPPING.

IT LOOKS LIKE IT'S GOING TO COME DOWN ALL DAY TODAY.

HOW COULD I, ON A DAY LIKE THIS...?

I MEAN, IT'S NOT LIKE I'VE EVER HAD LUCK ON MY SIDE...

IT'S AL- WAYS BEEN THIS WAY.

BUT I THOUGHT GOOD THINGS WERE FINALLY GOING TO START HAPPENING FOR ME...

A WHILE AGO...
I COULDN'T GET IN
BECAUSE I FORGOT
MY KEYS.

UH...

GO AHEAD AND EAT. I'LL FIX ME SOME-THING ELSE.

NO, IT'S OKAY.

THEN, HERE.

125

127

...BUT THAT WAS THEN AND THIS IS NOW. IF YOU DON'T WANT TO GO WITH ME, THAT'S FINE, BUT I'D LIKE YOU TO.

!!

I'll be first today.

IT'S SO ODD. HE'S NEVER BEEN THE TYPE TO SAY WHAT HE MEANS.

No, wait... I want to go with you.

FROM NOW ON, I CARRY YOUR BOOKS, TOO.

INSTEAD OF JUST TELLING ME THAT HE LIKES ME...

성큼 성큼

종종종

HE'S GOING TO SHOW IT WITH ACTION.

ARA, SIT HERE.

Move your leg, boy! And bathe ocasionally!

AT FIRST IT WAS WEIRD...

CAN I HAVE MY BAG BACK, PLEASE?

We're at school.

...BUT NOW I'D HAVE IT NO OTHER WAY!

Today I am a better man! Ho ho ho!

Picture 23.
A Crisis

IT'S MY FAULT, YOUNG-WOO, SO I'LL STAY AND HELP. IT'LL BE EASIER FOR TWO TO CLEAN.

WHEN I TOLD HIM I **WASN'T** ABSENT WITHOUT PRIOR NOTICE, HE GOT EVEN MORE MAD, AND NOW I HAVE TO CLEAN UP THE AUDITORIUM. IT'S SO UNFAIR.

DON'T WORRY. GIVE ME TEN MINUTES, AND I'LL BE SET.

TEN MINUTES? HOW'RE YOU GOING TO CLEAN THAT BIG AUDITORIUM IN JUST TEN MINUTES? C'MON, LET ME HELP.

DON'T WORRY. YOU GO HOME AND GET SOME REST.

IF SHE GOES HOME FIRST TO REST...

...THAT MEANS... THE TWO OF THEM... C-COULD IT BE?!!

YOU'D REALLY WANT TO LIVE WITH ARA AGAIN? WHAT BROUGHT THIS ON?

WHERE DO YOU COME UP WITH SUCH NONSENSE?

132

135

LET'S ASK HER TO COME BACK.

......

IT'S CLEAR TO ME NOW, YOUR BIOLOGICAL DAUGHTER ALWAYS COMES FIRST FOR YOU.

NO MATTER HOW GOOD SOMI AND I TREAT YOU, IT'LL NEVER MATTER.

137

142

144

IT'S THE BAKERY WHERE YOUNG-WOO BOUGHT THE CAKE...

NOW IT'S OUR BAKERY.

WOW... IT LOOKS DELICIOUS.

NOW THAT I THINK OF IT, YOUNG-WOO DIDN'T GET TO EAT ANY OF IT BEFORE MY FRIENDS SCARFED IT DOWN.

IN A FEW DAYS, IT WILL BE OUR 100-DAY ANNIVERSARY.

WE CAN HAVE AN ANNIVERSARY CELEBRATION! SWEET!

IT'S A GREAT IDEA.

YOUNG-WOO WILL LOVE IT, TOO. TEE HEE...

DAMN, IT'S FREEZING...WHAT'S TAKING THAT DITZY GIRL SO LONG?!

THANKS. I LOOK FORWARD TO SEEING WHAT YOU COME UP WITH. GOODBYE.

WHY AM I PUTTING MYSELF THROUGH THIS? TAKING MY NEMESIS DOWN BETTER BE WORTH IT

GRANDFATHER TOLD ME NOT TO TELL ARA, BUT...

...I MADE HER PROMISE TO TELL ME EVERYTHING...

HER FEELINGS WILL BE HURT IF SHE FINDS OUT I HID IT.

Ring
Ring

CAN'T COME TO THE PHONE Ring
RIGHT NOW...

WHY ISN'T SHE ANSWERING?

STOP IT!

STOP...

SHE'S AS FRUSTRATING AS EVER. SEE IF YOU CAN GET THROUGH.

ARA...SHE'S TELLING YOU THE TRUTH.

!!!

YOUR MARRIAGE WAS NEVER REGISTERED. HOW CAN YOU KEEP ON LIVING IN SIN?

TAXI

PLEASE ANSWER!!

THAT MAY BE...

I STILL...I WON'T GO.

I NEED TO TALK TO YOUNG-WOO ABOUT THIS. I'M NOT GOING TO MAKE ANY SNAP DECISIONS!

165

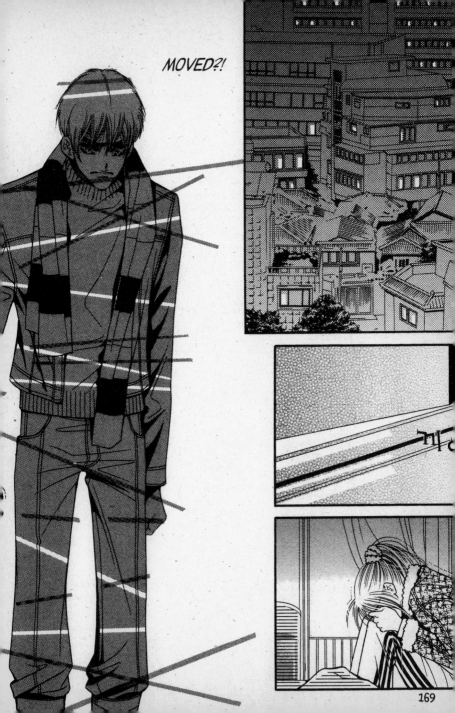

MOVED?!

169

171

Hello, everyone.

Today, I did charts for all four of the stars of *Honey Mustard*, to predict how their lives will be after they get married. Their astrological signs show how they will all fit together--I hope you will enjoy what this exercise reveals!

Khang Young-Woo: July 7th -- Leo

The male Leo behaves the same way in both business and love: He's a decisive, enthusiastic, compassionate provider who can make any girl happy. For example, he won't mind spending a little money to treat his girlfriend to a fancy dinner or lavish gift. But ladies beware--you may be overwhelmed by his volatile emotions!

Once he is married, the Leo makes an excellent husband and an exemplary father. But if things don't progress according to his wishes, he just may throw a temper tantrum! His flamboy-ant expressions of love are an indica-tor of his approach to life. If this man sets his heart on you, prepare to be pursued aggressively! He doesn't care whether he has a chance--he's going to try anyway.

Jung Hanil: June 8th -- Gemini

There is, of course, no perfect man... and our poor Gemini is one of those tragic types who can never fall completely in love. It's a common cliché that when tumbling in ecstasy with the object of your desire, even their faults will be beautiful to you...unless you're a Gemini, in which case you will see faults for what they are, and always reserve a corner in your heart to harbor doubt.

The typical Gemini man is intelligent while possessing the sort of masculine qualities that women adore. Yet he also has a cold streak, which makes him somewhat unapproachable. Although he dearly wants a relationship, he is very protective of his pride, and therefore doesn't pursue the ladies the way he should. Instead, he prefers a brave girl to approach him. He's not one to be tied down, and if more than one woman crosses his path at the same time, so much the better.

Go Ara: December 12th -- Sagittarius

The female Sag has a noble, clean, innocent aura. The purity of soul that she radiates makes her as beautiful as a flower in full bloom. Even in her forties she will seem ten years younger--and it will have nothing to do with physical appearance. This youthful beauty is the result of a joyful heart, and her high spirits will refresh those around her as well.

A smart and skillful wife, she can easily figure out what her husband is feeling and cheer him up when he is down. Because of this empathy, she will be a model wife and mother. As the center of her family, she spreads harmony among her neighbors and relatives. But she is especially diligent in assisting her mate, which will help him achieve success in other areas of life. Her uncanny perception lends itself to divining his work problems and delivering gentle words that will soothe his mind without bruising his ego. And if her husband is passive, she will show a surprising knack for taking charge and acting aggressively.

Go Somi: May 25th -- Gemini

The female Gemini has similar qualities to the male Gemini as a lover. She almost never allows herself to love completely, even if she has committed to the person in question. She does not cling to a partner, but remains totally self-reliant. So even if a Gemini girl is kissing you on the lips, she isn't losing herself in the moment. In fact, she's probably thinking about what she has to do tomorrow, or ruminating on your flaws.

If you do manage to convince a Gemini gal to walk down the aisle, her cool and objective nature will keep the union from becoming too volatile. However, the Gemini wife does have a tendency to compare her husband to other women's mates. Affection can soon turn to routine, leading to a rather humdrum lifestyle. But in the event that she finds the rarest of the rare--an ideal match--she will abandon herself completely and love her husband with gusto, surrendering her entire being to him. Could that lucky man be you?

TOKYOPOP SHOP

NO
LOITERING

© NARUMI SETO. © IG/VAP/NTV.

OTOGI ZOSHI
BY NARUMI SETO

An all-out samurai battle to retrieve the Magatama, the legendary gem that is said to hold the power to save the world!

Hot new prequel to the hit anime!

STRAWBERRY MARSHMALLOW
BY BARASUI

Cute girls do cute things...in *very* cute ways.

A sweet slice of delight that launched the delicious anime series!

© Barasui.

© SANAMI MATOH.

TRASH
BY SANAMI MATOH

When your uncle is the biggest mob boss in New York, it's hard to stay out of the family business!

From the creator of the fan-favorite *Fake!*

FOR THE BEST IN PAPERBACKS, LOOK FOR THE